Fly-Fishing in Southern New Mexico

Pool near head of Animas Creek

Fly-Fishing in Southern New Mexico

Rex Johnson Jr. and Ron Smorynski

University of New Mexico Press

Albuquerque

© 1998 by the University of New Mexico Press
Design by Mary Shapiro
Drawings © 1998 by Jay Scott
Photographs © 1998 by Michael P. Berman
All rights reserved.
First Edition

Library of Congress Cataloging-in-Publication Data

Johnson, Rex, 1950–
Fly-fishing in southern New Mexico / Rex Johnson, Jr. and
Ron Smorynski.—1st ed.
p.   cm.
Includes index.
ISBN 0-8263-1982-3   (paper)
1. Trout fishing—New Mexico.
2. Fly-fishing—New Mexico.
I. Smorynski, Ron, 1942-
II. Title.
SH688.U6J64   1998
799.1'757'09789—dc21   98-3952
                                         CIP

Contents

Maps

Illustrations

Drawings by Jay Scott

Photographs by Michael P. Berman

Acknowledgments

This book began as a sequence of articles on streams in the Sacramento Mountains for a possible second edition of the Sangre de Cristo Fly Fishers' *Fly-Fishing in Northern New Mexico,* whose safety information and basic format we have adopted. Rex Johnson wrote the introduction and description of the Gila watershed and other miscellaneous waters; Ron Smorynski authored the sections on the Sacramento Mountains, safety, state regulations, and small-stream fishing techniques; the section on trout species is a joint effort. George Sanders of Mesilla Valley Flyfishers described Quemado Lake and lakes in the Zuni Mountains. Retired Forest Service biologist Bill Zeedyk described Bluewater Creek and Lake. Bernardo Cerdan from Silver City assisted with lakes in the Gila. Richard Ramsay, a Ruidoso fishing guide, collaborated on the lakes in the Sacramento Mountains. Jerry Jacobi provided information on macro-invertebrates. Ti Piper, author of *Fishing in New Mexico,* gave information and encouragement. Bill Dunn, publisher of *Fishing New Mexico Monthly,* gave encouragement and permission to use published material.

Introduction

Rex Johnson, Jr.

"Yo voy caminando a la montaño donde naci."

I live in Silver City, New Mexico, 250 air miles east and slightly south of Phoenix, Arizona. Silver City lies at an altitude of 5,900 feet just below the reach of the forest, in the foothills of an isolated mountain range. During all my years in southwestern New Mexico, I never recall complaining about the weather. The ultraviolet light may be harsh in the thin atmosphere, but the sunshine is brilliant all year round. It is cool in winter and warm in summer, but always mild enough for being outdoors, and outdoors, in the mountains, is generally where I want to be. I have a very big back yard, in southern New Mexico.

Tourists show up in Silver City almost every month of the year, many looking for the flavor of the Old West in this century-old mining town. Billy Antrim, later known as Billy the Kid, New Mexico's most famous or infamous citizen, lived here for a time in the 1870s. Apache bands summered in the mountains nearby and raided cattle ranches, some of which employed Butch Cassidy and other colorful "outlaws. "

Less well known to tourists and locals alike are the trout streams in these same mountains. I have been fly-fishing for trout since June, 1965, almost year in and year out, from Sinaloa to the Northwest Territories, and I can hardly remember all the places I've fished. Yet most often I have found myself in the muntains above Silver City—somewhere on the Gila River or its forks, or the San Francisco, or any of dozens of others, smaller and harder to find. Butch Cassidy had his own hideout, and this has been mine, for nearly twenty years. It has been both goood and bad, but on the whole, I would say that it has been, for lack of a better word, excellent. I have been the luckiest of prospectors. Some of the streams I have fished are gone entirely, others as imperfectly remembered or greatly changed as the Old West itself. Time moves on and the mind fades. Yet, even so, nature itself remains forever young; there is still plenty left to enjoy. The fishing is still, for lack of a better word, excellent.

Among all the confusion, changes, and disappointments, some days in a fly-fisherman's career stand out in granular detail. One of the very best for me, out of hundreds, was spent in the Mogollon Mountains not far from Silver City on June 2, 1992. Here the light is so strong it hits you like a wave. Your eyes hurt. From ridgetops you can see over one hundred miles. The land literally glows. In the Mogollons, trees seek the shade and not the sun on the north sides of the peaks, spilling into the dark canyons. The south sides of the mountains are dull-colored and waterless, covered with low scrub and juniper trees. In the Mogollons this day, the air was cool but the sun still burned. I wore a sweat-stained baseball hat, sunglasses, and a long-sleeved, glowing white cotton shirt. My sandalled feet, already tanned like leather, had become sun-burned yet again. My tackle was sophisticated and expensive, but unnecessarily so. I could just has well have used my old fiberglass rod, which I still have, or even a cane pole—after all, as every fisherman knows, the child is the father of the man. I made a lot of casts that day, and nearly all brought trout; many were of a hybrid species native only to the Gila system, a river with hardly more flow than a grayling stream. It has always seemed odd to me that a drainage with such limited water could be home to a such a rich trout population. Today, in the Gila River's lower reaches, there is generally no water at all, and there are few or no trees. Yet not so long ago the whole lower river was a flowing, desert Eden, abounding in warmwater fishes, while in the higher mountain sources trout were everywhere. The trout, in particular, are so far from their original ancestral home it is remarkable they have found their way here. In this respect, I guess, they are a lot like me, and a lot like New Mexicans. The Gila River system, now so familiar to me, is truly in another world.

These pages contain a description of what the trout fishing was like in southern and central New Mexico as of 1995. What that will be like in ten or twenty years is anyone's guess. I first fished the Mogollon Mountains in 1977, and I wish I could step back in time and do it again. Whoever said "change is good" certainly was not a trout fisherman. Those who spend so much time looking into overlooked streams seem also to spend much of their time looking backwards, as their world becomes greatly altered and more crowded, with a smaller share of every good thing. There are, indeed, some things in this world that simply cannot be improved, any more than the circle can be squared. Fly-fishing for wild trout in natural surroundings, practiced essentially as it has been for centuries, is one of those. "Sane" is the Latin word for "whole," and there is no saner way to spend one's time, no pursuit of the mind more free of harm. It is, for lack of a better word, excellent.

Part I:
Background and Preparation

CHAPTER ONE

On the Edge of the Trout's World

Owing to complex patterns of mountains and weather, the western United States and northernmost Mexico contain some of the best trout habitats in the world. Native trout are found in this region far south of their original arctic homeland—in isolated pockets of the Southwest and all the way to the twenty-fourth parallel of north latitude. As a result, an angler can fish for trout ten months of the year in their original habitat near Silver City, just 80 air miles from Mexico.

The trout geography of New Mexico is quite easy to visualize. Clustered together in the north near the Colorado border are the Sangre de Cristo, San Juan, Tusas, and Jemez Mountain Ranges, plus a few outlying peaks and plateaus. These form the tag end of the southern Rocky Mountains, which in turn are part of a nearly unbroken chain of mountain ranges extending along the Continental Divide into western Canada and the Brooks Range of Alaska. Most of New Mexico's fly fishermen congregate in this part of the state.

South of Santa Fe, in the seemingly endless brown plains, creosote basins, and dry piñon ridges stretching to the south and on into old Mexico, trout are scarce. A fisherman can drive 200 miles and not see a single flowing stream. Yet trout are to be found in southern New Mexico. In the Sacramento Mountains—a rolling 8,000- to 9,000-foot-high land mass spreading south and east from the 12,000-foot peak of Sierra Blanca—you can find them. They do very well in several upper tributaries of the Bonito and Ruidoso Rivers, streams that drain eastward over the cholla grasslands and into the muddy Pecos. Immediately to the north, they are still hidden in the Capitan Mountains. Across the Estancia Basin, they have been planted on the back side of the Manzano Mountains. Someone even put them in the rugged Guadalupes of the Texas trans-Pecos, where the Rocky Mountains end and the Sierra Madre Oriental of Mexico begins. A few remnants of trout habitat survive in the Zuni Mountains south of Gallup.

Trout also flourish in New Mexico even farther off the beaten path. Tucked away in the southwestern corner of the state, and extending into Arizona, is a continuous mountain mass roughly 100 miles northwest to southeast and 60 miles northeast to southwest. Formerly known to the Spanish explorers as the Sierra del Gila, much of this *sierra,* like the Jemez Mountains to the north, is made up of the deeply eroded remains of an ancient field of volcanoes. Its eroded rim comprises,

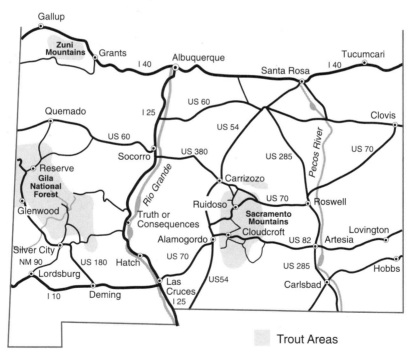

Fly-Fishing Southern New Mexico

essentially, the Mogollon, Tularosa, and San Francisco Mountains of New Mexico, as well as the Blue Range and White Mountains of neighboring Arizona. Nearby are fault block ranges like the east-adjoining Black Range, as well as the west-adjoining Pinaleños. As the earlier Spanish name implies, these mountains form the collective headwaters of the Gila River, the only major river arising and flowing entirely in what is now called the American Southwest.

There is no easy way to classify these mountains. They resemble, in parts, the Colorado Plateau, the Sierra Madre Occidental of Mexico, and the Basin and Range Province of inland California and Nevada, as well as the Rio Grande extension of the Rockies. Roughly three hundred streams here support wild populations of trout, and one-third of those lie on the New Mexico side. This mass of streams is one of the most isolated trout habitats in North America, now surrounded by 100 or more miles of desert and semi-desert stretching in all directions but the northwest, where the narrow green band of the Mogollon Plateau points toward the Grand Canyon. These waters vary from low-elevation canyons bordered by sycamore, cottonwood, box elder, and walnut to tiny springs issuing from rugged peaks nearly 11,000 feet above the sea, topped with aspen and spruce.

Abandoned by the Mimbreños and other pueblo dwellers by A.D. 1250, the region remained virtually unsettled until the end of the nineteenth century. Today nearly all of this land is within the public domain, still largely unsettled. The Sierra del Gila and the Mogollon Plateau are parceled into seven national forests and two Apache reservations. The New Mexico portion lies within the 3.3-million-acre Gila National Forest, second largest in the continental United States.

Even with federal oversight, however, many streams in the Gila region have been lost and many more are at risk. Under original climatic conditions, trout habitat had been contracting for perhaps ten thousand years. Due to the effects of recent land use, this contraction has accelerated over the last century, and many streams have lost trout populations. Others are severely degraded and on their way to that end.

East of Silver City, 40 miles out along the crest of the Black Range, just below 10,000-foot McKnight Peak—arriving, say, on a late August afternoon after the air has been scrubbed clean by a heavy monsoon thundershower—a trout fisherman can actually see nearly all the original trout-bearing mountains of southern New Mexico. Mounting the main north-south ridge on a two-rut forest service road to the Continental Divide, then standing on the highest ridge up there, he can see the Rio Grande valley and the San Andres Mountains to the east, over brown and barren slopes dropping off far below. Farther beyond, some 120 air miles away, lies the abrupt peak of Sierra Blanca. On its northern and eastern flanks, the Ruidoso and Bonito Rivers once held the large-spotted Pecos strain of the Rio Grande cutthroat trout. One transplanted population of Rio Grande cutthroats still survives in a tiny stream on the mountain's west slope, draining into the neighboring Tularosa Basin. Other Rio Grande cutthroats live closer at hand, in drainages about 3,500 feet nearly straight down to the east. These feed Las Animas Creek, which contains the southernmost surviving population of cutthroat trout of any kind.

Looking west from McKnight Mountain, over a loftier, forested landscape, the fisherman can oversee virtually the entire extant range of another distinct trout species. On the other side of the road, only 2,500 hundred feet below in McKnight Canyon, lives the Gila trout, the only full-fledged trout species listed as "endangered." Immediately beyond, the west slope of the Black Range held 50 percent of the world's population of these fish as recently as 1989. The plants, insects, birds, and other terrestrial and aerial beings are virtually identical on either side of McKnight Mountain, but the Gila trout on the left and the Rio Grande cutthroat on the right have never left the confines of their slender streams of water; they remain separate and distinct, after anywhere from one hundred thousand to one million years of evolutionary change.

Farther to the west rises the transverse, southeast-to-northwest ridge of the Pinos Altos Range, and beyond it the main peaks of the roadless Mogollons—Sacaton Mountain, Mogollon Baldy, the whale's head shape of Willow Mountain, and the hard-to-see knob top of the highest peak, 10,876-foot Whitewater Baldy. This is the heart of the Gila country, the headwaters of the Gila River. Most of the remaining Gila trout are scattered among those peaks; hybrids—nearly identical to the pure-strain populations—live there, too, along with the usual assortment of rainbows, browns and, in one peculiar stream, brook trout.

Fishing these waters is like taking a glimpse back at the created world in one of its little-known corners. The highest streams of this range are truly tiny and often far apart. Sometimes it does not rain for over a month at a time, even during a normal year. During a dry year the streams all but disappear.

One hundred miles farther away on the western horizon looms the isolated Mount Graham in Arizona, an ancient forest refuge as high as the Mogollons, all alone and hazy blue. To its left are pine-clad Cochise Head and the spruce-topped Chiricahua Mountains, the northern tip of the 1,000-mile-long Sierra Madre Occidental. You can see the 9,900-foot height of Chiricahua Peak, just below which lies the southernmost trout stream in the United States. Far to the right, inhabiting the most northern slopes of this far-away, cloud-like land mass is yet another fish species, once called the Arizona but now renamed the Apache trout. Like the Arizona alder, Arizona sycamore, and Arizona walnut, the Arizona trout is in fact native to New Mexico, in the Blue River and Dry Blue Creek, which join together just east of the state line.

What did this grand view look like two hundred years ago? In October 1846, as the advance guard of Stephen Kearny's Army of the West approached the unmapped Black Range of what is now southern New Mexico, Lt. William Emory stepped over a small, clear stream whose flow was roughly as big around as a man's waist. As men, horses, and mules stopped to drink and fill water buckets, Emory looked around. It was a golden, blue day, like all the others, the sun warm and the air cool. It had not rained for a month. He climbed back down into a canyon bottom to make his way over the mesas and toward the big ridges looming to the west. His glance at the creek was only one of many steps made during that particular day, but he duly recorded it in his journal, noting the "clear, limpid and cool" water. Had he taken time to look carefully into the stream, parting the willows and grass which kept it nearly hidden and peering into pockets of deeper current under the banks, he might have spotted a native cutthroat trout, but he was in a hurry.

Today the land is so greatly changed that it is hard to determine exactly where he was at that particular moment, or exactly what he saw that day. He soon crossed another stream of the same size. The next day he noted a country that was "traversed by small streams of pure water." Perhaps it was Palomas Creek he first saw, and then Seco, Animas, Middle or South Percha, Trujillo or Berenda Canyon. Today these are only names; there is no stream of any kind flowing in October from the Black Range to the Rio Grande. The same river bluffs and bench lands where Kearny found grass for hundreds of horses and mules on the evening of 15 October 1846, today have creosote shrubs, old mining anthills spilling into dry arroyos, tumbledown sheds, a house trailer or two, cactus, sand, and dust.

The three trout species remaining in this crossroads within a 60-mile range—the Gila, Apache, and Rio Grande cutthroat trout—are the only true sport fish native to New Mexico, along with the Colorado cutthroats *(Oncorhynchus clarki pleuriticus)* of the Chuska Mountains and the large-mouth bass of the Pecos. The bass remain, but the Gila and Rio Grande trout are in jeopardy; the others disappeared from here entirely many years ago. Most New Mexicans, even avid fly fishermen, have never seen any of the state's native trout. In place of the unique forms which evolved here over the ages, we have seen a domestic menagerie of hatchery-bred rainbow trout; northern pike; smallmouth, largemouth, spotted, and striped bass; brown trout; arctic grayling; lake trout; and kokanee, chinook, and coho salmon.

The basic fertility and southerly latitude of the streams in southern New Mexico provide the potential for trout to grow and prosper almost year-round, provided water temperatures stay sufficiently cool. Accordingly, the original trout distribution in the mountains of the region consisted simply of all the higher streams that didn't dry up during normal weather cycles, or that normally flowed uninterruptedly into permanent cold water. Since all rivers in southern New Mexico flow quickly into hot semi-arid regions and have done so for the past several thousand years, any isolated stream system which loses its water during severe drought can never, under natural conditions, regain trout. Fires, as well as drought, can remove trout from a stream.

To hold trout over the millennia, a mountain watershed must not only contain permanent streams, but must also be extensive and complex. Such watersheds in southern New Mexico seem to have been limited to the upper-elevation Gila and San Francisco River systems near the Arizona–New Mexico border, draining the Mogollon Mountain complex and eastern slopes of Sierra Blanca and the Sacramento Range— precisely those ranges that can be seen from atop McKnight Mountain. Historical records of the Gila River system indicate that trout inhabited waters of perhaps 4,000 feet in elevation and higher as recently as the late nineteenth century. So an historical picture of where trout fishing *should* be in southern New Mexico is easy to visualize.

Where the trout actually *are* today is trickier. For instance, of the roughly 1,000 miles of permanently flowing water remaining in the Gila Forest, only 250 miles or so hold trout populations of any significance, while an additional 300 miles hold smaller numbers. Streams with trout can still be found at an elevation of 5,000 feet or more, wherever there is a reliable permanent flow coupled with essentially natural conditions, where the overlying watershed has a healthy mantle of trees and grass, and the stream banks have a riparian plant community sheltering the water.

The mountains of southern New Mexico were never heavily timbered, except at the very highest elevations. When the first forest reserves were designated in 1899, most of the mountains were open woodland and grassy savannah. Many lower basins in the region were almost entirely without trees, sloping toward bottoms supporting either permanent, grassy streams, with open swales of sacaton grass, or, wherever the shallow water table reached the surface, wet meadows, or *cienegas*. During the rainy season a mosaic of upland "bunch" grasses grew green and tall, knee-high, often waist-high; then, during the dry fall the grass dried, lightened in the sun, and fell back in a protective mulch layer, helping to keep subsoil moisture intact.

Today, one glance over the lower slopes and upland mesas of the same region reveals a scanty growth of grass a quarter-inch or so high over dry, exposed ground, or no grass at all. Much of the subsurface water has been drained away, the water table in the dry bottoms now far below the reach of the plants. It looks very much like desert. The lower slopes of the mountains have literally changed color, from a golden light-burnished yellow—the color of fall prairie and winter wheat—to a dull reddish brown, the color of exposed volcanic rock, soil, and rubble. Evergreen shrubs and brush thickets now cover higher, mid-elevation slopes and pour down into the draws and ravines; juniper have "invaded" the mesas, with an understory of extremely sparse grass and exotic weeds. The ground-level vegetation in many places has become "discrete"; that is to say, the plants are separated by bare sand and earth, which is one definition of true desert cover. Protected from fires, the pockets of timber on some of the higher reaches are now thicker and crowded with younger trees, a "dog hair" growth leaving little except dead needles on the ground beneath.

The reasons for this change are clear. Grazing pressure has had considerable impact on what might be called "natural conditions" and has been felt nearly everywhere in the region for many years. Grass relentlessly eaten away by cattle over long periods of time becomes progressively weakened and eventually disappears. Plants avoided by cattle—because they find them either distasteful or mildly toxic—remain. Over time these lowly, overlooked plants, formerly unable to compete with the grass for moisture and space, are now found to be better able to grow. Eventually they replace the grasses that once mastered over them, nature abhorring a complete vacuum. Thus, over time, weeds, scrub forest, and brush are found to have replaced the grasslands over the entire landscape. All of this has happened over the past ninety years, and it is still happening. Virtually all the plants you see growing over much of today's completely altered range are simply the various sizes of all the weeds that cows do not eat, from the juniper tree on down.

This change in appearance also reflects the different ways in which water either evaporates, seeps into the ground, or else moves across the surface and drains away; and, accordingly, profound changes are evident in any number of the streams. Many smaller rivers and larger creeks which were once permanent now lose most or all of their flow during the seven dry months of the year. One notable example of this is the Diamond Creek system of the western slope of the Black Range, which held tens of thousands of Gila trout in no less than four of its major branches as recently as 1938. The trout population of this entire system plummeted to eighty or so individual fish in 1991, in one of the few stretches of the drainage that had not dried up entirely.

Before the turn of the century virtually the entire Gila River watershed above 4,700 feet contained pure populations of Gila trout, including a blue-ribbon fishery of perhaps six thousand or more mature trout per mile in the mainstem, a relatively small stream with summer flow of 70 to 100 cubic feet per second (cfs). Trout in the Gila mainstem were at least as abundant then as warm-water suckers and minnows are in those same waters today, perhaps much more so. At the same time, waters from 4,000 to 4,700 feet in elevation contained mixed populations of trout and warm-water fish. Today, by contrast, the entire mainstem of the Gila River contains proportionately few trout. I would hazard a guess that fewer than 1 percent of the fish in the river's main stem above 4,700 feet consist of these cold-water species. Even the upper forks of the Gila, noted throughout the state for their fishing as recently as the 1950s, today do not hold pure, or in some cases even significant, populations of stream-born trout below 7,000 feet.

Most streams in the forest bear little resemblance to their former selves, but some do. Today's differences are quite easy to see in the water itself and may be traced to a scarcity of riparian grasses, trees, and other plants. A good stream has good water quality, clean spawning redds, and plentiful organic input, 90 percent of which consists of leaf litter and other plant material grown on the banks and slopes outside the water itself. A poor trout stream is either too warm, too dirty, or lacking in food. Streamside plant cover provides food and cools the water; upland vegetation prevents silting and keeps water clean. Trout are plant dependent.

Streams in southern New Mexico have an enormous ratio of watershed area to flow volume, which means that rainfall has to travel a long way, both above and below the ground, before reaching the bed of a permanent stream. Large source springs are rare. A waist-deep pool represents an enormously broad accumulation of scarce water over a watershed the size of one of the smaller national parks. A shoulder-deep pool often represents the net product of a watershed of 200,000 acres or more. Under these conditions, subtle but widespread ground disturbances become concentrated many times before being reflected in the way the stream functions and in the purity and temperature of its water—both crucial factors for trout.

Of particular importance is temperature, since the Gila River system is not terribly far from the southernmost natural occurrences of trout in the world. Disturbances in the riparian forest canopy along both permanent and semi-permanent streams can quickly send summer water temperatures over the limits for trout. For instance, the air temperature under the shade of the dense willow–cottonwood *bosque* that once lined most rivers can be as much as 15 degrees cooler than the ambient temperature above the forest. When this shade is removed, the sun's energy directly warms the stream. No water near the southern and downstream limits for trout can absorb any part of the 15-degree increase in air temperature that the removal of this canopy would represent. Furthermore, rainfall in the Gila watershed varies wildly, both during the year and from year to year. Half the yearly precipitation comes as violent thunderstorm downpours in July and August, a condition which further magnifies the effects of ground disturbance and stream impacts. There is also up to 400 percent variation in annual precipitation within a normal ten-to-fifteen-year climatic cycle, with both flood and drought a normal part of the cycle. All of these factors amount to shock treatment for area trout streams, even under pristine, natural conditions. When these conditions are altered, the shock is all the greater, and the streams sometimes simply disappear.

When vegetation disappears, rain bleeds the soil away, floods occur, and the blown-apart stream gradually dies. Most rivers in the Southwest today look like broad sandy washes, most often with little or no water at the bottom. They function merely as gutters. Often the stream channel seems to be designed for a tremendous flow, but also seems oddly overdesigned, for it sits generally empty—bone dry. Only a few times a year will the gutter come to life; suddenly a muddy torrent will rush through the basin, putting the gouged-out stream bottom to temporary use before either filling a reservoir, evaporating, or sinking into desert sands. This is not the way area rivers were originally meant to be.

Nineteenth- and early-twentieth-century reports of flood conditions on trout streams like the upper Gila River and Tonto Creek in neighboring Arizona frequently mentioned that before the decline of the grazing ranges and the removal of the dense river *bosques,* high spring flood waters moved gently, filling tree-rimmed marshes along the flood plain. Much of the current was diverted around flood-filled, broad lagoons. These lagoons and sloughs gradually dried and drained over the course of the summer, leaving low-lying ponds and providing a nursery for myriads of cottonwood and other well-suited deciduous tree seedlings, fishes, (including trout), birds, aquatic insects, amphibians, and other larger wildlife. Only today can floods be called "destructive."

In summary, the quantity and quality of vegetation is what largely determines the health and productivity of each stream; this has been altered by, and is still dependent upon, man. On the public lands of southern New Mexico, where nearly all trout waters arise and flow, vegetative quality today is determined by land management practices.

These practices vary greatly and are principally characterized by the rates at which cattle are stocked. These rates are, as a rule, the most important factor in choosing between good and bad places to fish— the lower the rate, the better the prospects. A few streams such as Rio Bonito at Fort Stanton and Agua Chiquita Creek in the Lincoln National Forest have streamside grazing restrictions. In the Gila National Forest, by contrast, nearly the entire portion of the Gila Wilderness west of the Cliff Dwellings Highway is off-limits to cattle. It is in such specially managed areas as these that the best habitat and best fishing occur. Note well.

CHAPTER TWO

Trout of Southern New Mexico

Native Trout of Southern New Mexico

Three types of trout were originally found in southern New Mexico: the Gila trout, the Arizona or Apache trout, and two strains of the Rio Grande cutthroat trout. The Arizona trout occupied only a tiny portion of New Mexico within the Blue River watershed. The other natives have virtually disappeared and, with one exception, cannot even be fished for today. Understanding a little bit about these trout, however, helps one better understand what the background and essential limitations of trout fishing might be in this semi-arid and unlikely landscape.

Rio Grande Cutthroat

The Rio Grande cutthroat, *Oncorhynchus clarki virginalis,* was seen by Coronado in the year 1541 in Glorieta Creek near Santa Fe making this species the first trout in North America to be described by Europeans. Both Coronado and subsequent Spanish travelers, well acquainted with the native brown trout of Europe, noted the abundance and fine table qualities of the brown's New World counterparts. The evident range of the *virginalis* was originally the Rio Grande watershed of southern Colorado and northern New Mexico, the headwaters of the Pecos and Canadian River drainages in New Mexico, plus isolated higher-elevation streams in other parts of the Rio Grande drainage, including nineteenth-century reports of populations in the Davis

Mountains and upper Devils River watershed in Texas. In southern New Mexico this broad range included the Rio San Jose system draining the Zuni Mountains, Tijeras Canyon, the eastern slope of the Sacramento Mountains, and the Black Range near Silver City. The Sacramento Mountain population were part of the so-called Pecos strain of the Rio Grande cutthroat, with extra large, dime-sized black spots.

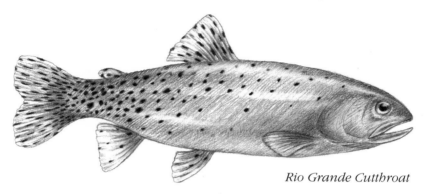

Rio Grande Cutthroat

Only two populations of pure or relatively pure Rio Grande cutthroats still exist in southern New Mexico. One is in Indian Creek on the Mescalero Apache Indian Reservation and is closed to angling, the other is in the headwaters of Las Animas Creek. The New Mexico Department of Game and Fish (NMG&F) is developing a program to restore Rio Grande cutthroat trout, so more waters may have them in the future.

The Rio Grande subspecies is among the most colorful of the cutthroats. It is distinguished by two red or orange slashes on its lower jaw and a vivid, greenish blue wash on its back. Some fish also display rich, reddish orange coloration on the opercle and belly, especially colorful on breeding males. The spotting pattern is distinctive, with large, dark, irregular spots concentrated in front of the tail fin. Spots on the forward part of the body are scattered and are found primarily above the lateral line. Rio Grande cutthroat spawn in the spring, triggered by warming water that signals the end of the spring runoff, allowing the eggs and sacfry to develop when the oxygen content of the water in the gravel is still high.

Cutthroats are opportunistic feeders and are rightly considered the easiest of the trout to catch. They feed primarily on aquatic invertebrates and terrestrial insects. There is a two-fish limit on cutthroats in New Mexico. **Because of their rarity and susceptibility to angling pressure, all cutthroats should be released.**

Gila Trout

In a 1939 issue of *New Mexico Magazine,* Glenwood Hatchery manager Edwin Shelley had the following to say about the native trout of southwestern New Mexico:

> *We have a kind of trout here in the Mogollon Mountains called the West Slope Native which is not found anywhere else except the Gila River drainage. Until this spring they were unknown to anyone except the New Mexico and Arizona game departments, the U.S. Forest Service, and the local people in this territory. In March, 1939, we sent a number of fish to Washington, D. C. for classification. Not only are they very beautiful and gamey fish, but they are far better suited to this territory than any other trout.*

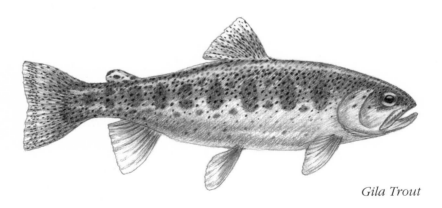

Gila Trout

> *We have some pretty good streams in the southwestern part of the state, but many of them are small and portions of some dry up during the dry seasons. There is also quite a change in water temperature throughout the year in the small streams. The West Slope*

Native has adapted itself to these conditions. In the smaller streams they never leave the pools that have permanent water, even though water runs high during the rainy seasons; therefore the loss of fish that become trapped in the pools that go dry is very small. Also, they are better able to stand the wide range of temperatures and the extreme low waters. We have on hand now about sixteen hundred of these trout for brood stock and plan to raise enough to restock most of the streams in this section of the state with this native species. In this way we hope to create more satisfactory fishing conditions since there is no doubt but that the West Slope Native will survive and reproduce better under existing erratic conditions than any other species.

This was the Gila trout, *Oncorhynchus gilae,* native to the upper Gila and San Francisco watersheds, which Shelley and his crew raised at the Glenwood hatchey from 1939 until 1947. The species had originally existed in pure populations in the Gila River system upstream from the town of Cliff and extending as far downstream as the present-day community of Redrock, mixed with native warm-water species at 4,000 feet. Arizona populations are believed to have occupied parts of the upper Verde River watershed, and perhaps also Eagle Creek, near Clifton, Arizona.

Today the Gila trout is endangered, and only about a dozen accepted pure populations exist in the headwaters of small streams, all closed to fishing. At present the Gila Trout Recovery Team is trying to increase the species' remaining range and numbers in hopes of "downlisting" them to threatened status, which will allow some angling for this rare trout.

Gila trout are a subtly colored fish, of a soft golden yellow, darker along the back and head, sometimes shading to an olive brown in these areas among large adults, with a faint rosy "redband" along the sides. Fine black spots are sprinkled generously over the upper body, dorsal fin, and tail, while the lower fins run yellow to orange, with milky white tips—often with orange colors near the fin attachments on the belly and lower body. There is a faint mustard yellow "cutthroat" mark under the jaw, and the gill covers are brassy to reddish orange. Several roughly elliptical purple bars are arranged vertically across the side, growing fainter with age and becoming a faint purple-silver iridescent sheen in large adults. Seen at a glimpse, the fish appears merely golden yellow and finely spotted. Smaller fish up to 10 inches also show their purple bars, or parr marks, quite clearly. The largest known specimen, caught in the West Fork of the Gila River in the 1930s, was between 21 and 22 inches in length. The Gila and Apache trout are so similar that some taxonomists consider them the same species.

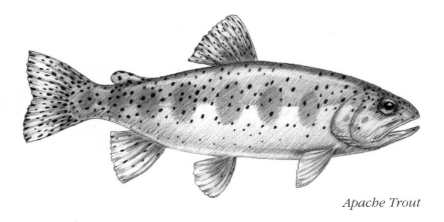

Apache Trout

The Gila is a spring spawner and seems to feed in opportunistic fashion strictly on insects—primarily stonefly and mayfly naiads and caddisfly larvae, less frequently on terrestrial insects. It seems to be tolerant of warm water up to 80 degrees, and is also tolerant of high seasonal floods.

Because no one can fish for Gila trout, little is said about these "West Slope Natives" today. Fishermen do catch a few outside the closed areas, as well as the hybrids common in many streams. At present all captured Gila trout must be released unharmed. Protected populations live in Spruce, upper Big Dry, upper Little, upper Iron, Main Diamond, upper Mogollon, upper White, Sheep Corral, McKenna, South Diamond, and Sacaton Creeks, and McKnight and Trail Canyons. (All the streams listed as "upper" are open to normal fishing below a waterfall or man-made barrier.)

The Gila trout interbreeds readily with both cutthroats and rainbows, producing fertile hybrid offspring. Many thousands of both Gila and rainbow trout were stocked in southwestern New Mexico from the turn of the century until the 1940s. Accordingly, the Gila-rainbow hybrid is in all likelihood the most common wild trout in the Gila Forest, having replaced the Gila trout in most of the latter's ancestral habitat in the Mogollon Mountains. Found in both the upper reaches of most trout waters and also in stream sections generally too warm to support browns, most of these hybrids resemble rainbows, yet with faint purple oblong blotches, or "parr marks" along the sides and a yellowish or brassy body color.

Trout Introduced to Southern New Mexico

Rainbow Trout

The rainbow, *Oncorhynchus mykiss,* is a native species almost exclusively of Pacific Coast drainages ranging from Alaska's Bristol Bay to northern Baja California. Two populations of native rainbow or para-rainbow trout also occur in mainland Mexico near the twenty-fourth parallel. Their habitat is essentially a narrow band, 500 miles or less from the Pacific, stretching from the subarctic to the subtropics—not really a large North American range. The reason for this is simply that the continent's Pacific drainages are quite short, owing to the westward movement of the continent and the eons-old piling of major mountain masses on its leading edge. As a result, the rainbow has never occurred very far from the Pacific Ocean. This limited natural range contrasts with the fish's propagation by man all over the globe, in both northern and southern hemispheres, owing mainly to the ease with which it is now raised in hatcheries.

Massive plantings of hatchery rainbows in the Mogollon and White Mountains in the last fifty years have resulted in a wild, nondescript population of rainbow-Gila and rainbow–Apache trout hybrids that have all but eliminated these native species. The hybrids, as mentioned above, are well adapted and compete favorably with the introduced browns.

Hatchery rainbows are also planted as "catchables" in some of the larger streams and in a handful of very small reservoirs across southern New Mexico. Naturalized rainbow populations inhabit the Sacramento, Zuni, and Manzano Mountains of New Mexico, and have even adapted to one stream in the Guadalupe Mountains of trans-Pecos Texas on the New Mexico border.

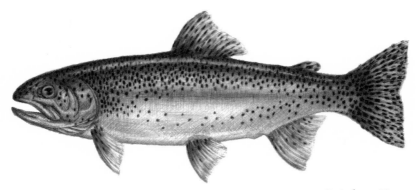

Rainbow Trout

Several streams in the Sacramento Mountains contain reproducing populations of rainbows with some cutthroat trout influence, possibly inherited from the original Rio Grande cutthroats once found here. You'll be tipped off by orange blotches on the belly of a cutthroat-rainbow hybrid (cutbow). Orange coloration on the opercle can be found on some cutbows, and light red or yellowish orange slashes either side of the lower jaw are other indicators. Hybrids don't dominate large portions of any stream but do well in several areas. The Rio Bonito has a population in its headwaters above Bonito Lake (including the South Fork) and there is also a good population downstream near the town of Lincoln. Upper Eagle Creek and Tularosa Creek have populations. In the southern part of the Sacramentos, the Rio Peñasco and Sacramento Rivers also have these hybrids (fire in 1994, however, may have killed all rainbows in the Sacramento).

Rainbows are the most popular trout in southern New Mexico because they are easy and inexpensive to raise, easy for novice fishermen to catch with bait, and because they are known for their fighting spirit—rainbows seem to swim faster and leap more often. First stocked in southern New Mexico in Bluewater and Eagle Creeks in 1896, they have since been put into virtually all major streams at one time or another. The New Mexico Department of Game and Fish stocks most public waters; the U.S. Fish and Wildlife Service plants them on the Mescalero Apache Reservation, and they are also stocked privately.

The top of the head, back, and upper sides are brownish to bluish green with numerous small dark spots. The sides are silvery, with a pink to reddish strip often evident along the lateral line. The dorsal, caudal, and adipose fins have dark spots.

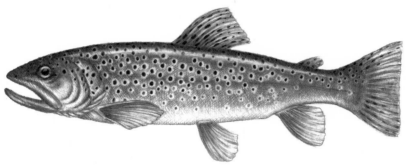

Brown Trout

Brown Trout

Brown trout, *Salmo trutta,* are the most exotic of the salmonids introduced into southern New Mexico, originally found west of the Ural Mountains in Russia and ranging to the Caspian Sea, the Atlas Mountains of North Africa, and up through Spain, the British Isles, Iceland, and Scandinavia. They were first introduced into the United States in 1883 and into New Mexico in 1892. In southern New Mexico, wild browns inhabit the middle to high elevations of the Mogollons in streams like the Middle and West Forks of the Gila River, Black Canyon, and Iron,

Big Dry, Mogollon, and Willow Creeks. They are also found in such Sacramento Mountain waters as the Rio Peñasco, most of the Rio Ruidoso, the lower part of the Rio Bonito, and Tularosa, Carrizo, and Cedar Creeks. Some brown trout fry are stocked in streams by the NMG&F from time to time. Adults are olive brown with a golden tint, with large black and small reddish orange spots on the sides. The belly is yellow or cream colored.

Browns predominate in larger, lower-gradient streams, provided the water remains cool. They spawn in the fall, which gives excellent results where late fall or winter floods and spring runoff don't destroy the eggs or fry. Even in streams where brown trout normally dominate, there can be major drops in population after winter floods or high spring runoff. Summer floods normally have less effect. Browns are a favorite of fly fishers because they feed more selectively, they are easily frightened, and once disturbed they wait longer then other trout before feeding again.

Brook Trout

Brook Trout, *Salvelinus fontinalis,* are native to eastern Canada and the northeastern United States, with this central range extending southward from the top of the Appalachians to northern Georgia, and to the Great Lakes and a few headwater tributaries of the Mississippi in Minnesota and Wisconsin. They were introduced into southern New Mexico in the early 1900s.

Brook trout are chars and have the inverse coloration of trout—light-colored spots on a dark background. Patterns on their backs resemble drawings of worms, background color varies from light silvery blue to dark green. Red areas are often ringed with halos of yellow or off-white. The lower fins are reddish orange with white leading edges. In shaded water, brook trout have bright colors and are among our most beautiful fish, especially males during the fall spawning period. In more sunlit waters they have a washed-out look, causing some anglers to confuse them with brown trout.

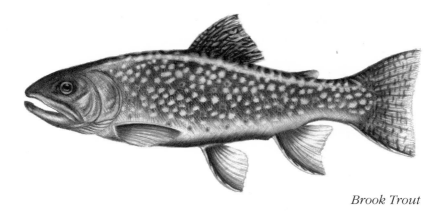

Brook Trout

Brookies do better in smaller, colder waters and will spawn in springs, which gives them an advantage in small streams and some lakes. This characteristic serves them particularly well in the southern part of the Sacramento Mountains, where many streams are so rich in calcium that a heavy caliche cements the bottom gravel together. They also seem to be able to live through low-water conditions. They predominate in the Sacramento River, Agua Chiquita, Eagle, and Three Rivers Creeks. Other streams with populations include the Rio Bonito and the headwaters of the Rio Ruidoso, as well as tiny Argentina Canyon, Copeland Canyon, Pine Lodge Creek, Big Bear Creek, and Little Bear Canyon. The only watershed with brook trout in the Gila is Whitewater Creek, whose South Fork offers excellent brook trout fishing.

Brook trout are easy to catch on flies if you don't scare them first. A cautious approach to the water is especially important on the small clear streams found in southern New Mexico.

CHAPTER THREE

Fishing Regulations and Fishing Safety

New Mexico Fishing Regulations

Anglers in New Mexico over the age of 12 must have a license to fish. Current yearly fees are $17.50 for residents; $10.50 for a junior, senior, or handicapped license; and $39 for nonresidents. Short-term licenses of one or five days are also available. Statewide, there is a daily limit of six trout, or two cutthroat trout, with lower limits on Special Trout Waters. At present, streams or stream reaches known to contain pure Gila trout are closed to fishing. For specific regulations, read the New Mexico Fishing Proclamation, available with the purchase of a license or at Department of Game and Fish offices.

The New Mexico Department of Game and Fish (NMG&F) has implemented the Sikes Act throughout the state. The act requires anglers and hunters who use public land managed by the Bureau of Land Management (BLM) and the U.S. Forest Service to buy a habitat improvement stamp costing $5.25. Money from sale of the stamps is used for habitat improvement projects on lands managed by the two agencies. Because the majority of fishing waters described in this book are located on public land, anglers should purchase the stamp with each fishing license.

On New Mexico's Special Trout Waters, angling is usually limited to flies and lures with single, barbless hooks, and bag limits are lower. Presently, the only Special Trout Waters in southern New Mexico are small sections of Gilita Creek and the Rio Ruidoso, which have limits of two trout. There are no catch-and-release waters in southern New Mexico, but any trout suspected of being a Gila trout must be released alive.

The use of boats on any water in New Mexico must conform to the regulations of the New Mexico Boat Act, administered by the New Mexico State Park and Recreation Division, P.O. Box 1147, Santa Fe, NM 87504-1147; phone (505) 827-7465. Float tubes are allowed and boats are restricted to oars or electric motors at Bear Canyon Lake, Bill Evans Lake, Lake Roberts, Quemado Lake, McGaffey Lake, Snow Lake, and Wall Lake. Boats and float tubes are not allowed at Bonito Lake. At Ramah Lake boats may be used at trolling speeds only. Privately owned boats or float tubes may not be used on waters at Mescalero Lake, but the Inn of the Mountain Gods rents boats for use at the lake. To use a boat without a motor or a float tube at Grindstone Lake, a $5 per day permit must be purchased from the city of Ruidoso.

Do not fish on private land without written permission! Under New Mexico state law anyone convicted of such an act can lose hunting and fishing rights for three years.

Fishing Safety

Climate, Temperature, Weather, and Seasons
Fly-fishing in comfort can be pursued year-round in southern New Mexico. The weather is normally sunny and dry. On some streams in winter, anglers can even fish in shirt sleeves during mild weather. The higher elevations can be cool enough for pleasant fishing most of the day in summer, but anglers must be aware that on any day the normal temperature swing is 30 to 40 degrees. Appropriate clothing and rain-wear should be available.

Summers in the mountains are warm, with daily temperatures reaching the 80s and 90s, and occasionally 100 degrees; yet the nights are cool. At lower elevations, winters are mild but variable, with highs in the 60s during warm spells and the 30s during cold spells. Remember, temperatures will drop about 5 degrees for each 1,000 feet of ascent.

In addition, at any time of year sudden thunderstorms can lower temperatures by 20 to 30 degrees in a matter of minutes. Anglers caught away from shelter in the mountains risk hypothermia unless they have suitable clothing and rainwear.

In winter, the air temperature may remain above freezing most of the day, but will drop below freezing at night, after the sun disappears behind the mountains. Fishing with dry flies during *Baetis* hatches is possible almost all winter. Water temperatures in winter are often frigid, and anglers must be aware that getting soaked can lead to hypothermia, especially during windy conditions. Know the weather forecast before beginning a winter fishing trip. Winter storms can descend fast, lowering temperatures 25 degrees in an hour and filling the air with snow. When heading for the Gila in winter, take plenty of warm clothing, insulated waders or hip boots (preferably neoprene), blankets, matches, hot drinks, and a complete set of dry clothes.

Springtime temperatures make for great fly-fishing, but the numerous windy fronts can make things difficult. The winds are the strongest from 10 A.M. to 5 P.M., which is when most people are on the stream, so get out early and stay late. Take a break during the middle of the day. A few of these fronts produce rain and snow.

Summer fishing is pleasant in the mountains, although it can get up to 100 degrees on some lower-elevation streams in the afternoon. The mornings and evenings are cool, and it is necessary to carry a light jacket for comfort. Mornings are usually clear, but by noon large thunderheads often build up, producing afternoon thundershowers that can be accompanied by hail and severe lightning. Usually of short duration, the storms can be intense and quite violent. Even in summer the temperature during a storm at our many high-elevation trout streams can drop to 30 degrees. Anglers without rainwear and warm clothing can easily get into trouble. New Mexico also has a high number of lightning strikes each year, and anglers should seek shelter during thunderstorms. Don't stand under large trees in the open; look for a stand of small trees to stand under. Rainwear is a necessary part of the summer fly fisherman's equipment. When packing in wilderness areas in summer it's best to do all traveling in the morning and have a camp set up by noon. This way you can rest when temperatures get high, or take cover in your tent if it rains.

Hypothermia

Most deaths in the backcountry are caused by exposure, or hypothermia. This is the dangerous cooling of the body's core temperature. The symptoms are uncontrollable shivering, stiff muscles, painful hands and feet, slurred speech, slowed heartbeat, poor coordination, and stumbling. Even in the wilderness the mild stages of hypothermia are easily treated. Get dry and put on extra, dry clothing, including a hat. Get into a sleeping bag with somebody.

Sun Protection

A problem resulting from New Mexico's abundant sunshine and thin atmosphere is a high incidence of skin cancer. This is worse for fly fishermen because they spend so much time standing within the water's reflective surface. Fishermen should wear long-sleeved shirts and wide-brimmed hats. It is also necessary to apply sunscreen with a rating of at least 20 SPF to face, lips, ears, and hands before starting the day's fishing; don't wait until your skin turns red. If you choose to wear insect repellent, apply it after the sunblock. It is also essential to wear sunglasses that block at least the sun's ultraviolet rays. Inadequate eye protection can result in burned retinas or painfully sore eyes after a day's fishing in the sun's glare.

Altitude Sickness

Higher elevations also mean lower concentrations of oxygen, making hiking and wading more difficult, even exhausting. When fishing in the mountains, slow down and avoid heavy exertion. Rapid ascents to high elevations can lead to mountain sickness, whose symptoms include headache, nausea, weakness, shortness of breath, and general aching; discomfort is usually worse in the morning. A gradual ascent into the mountains, with time spent at an intermediate altitude, will help reduce the possibility of this condition. If the symptoms do occur, dropping to a lower elevation will usually relieve them. If the symptoms persist, get medical assistance.

Dehydration

When fishing in dry southern New Mexico, you must drink plenty of fluids to prevent dehydration. Be prepared to drink at least a gallon each day. Don't drink water directly from the stream; it may contain *Giardia,* a protozoan that causes a severe intestinal disorder. Either carry water or purify water from the stream by boiling, use of chemicals, or filtering. Check with backpacking stores for information on filters and chemicals to purify water.

Snakes

Rattlesnakes are common during the warm months along streams. Particularly in the morning and evening, keep a sharp lookout for snakes while walking the banks of streams. As a simple precaution when walking or climbing, always check for snakes before placing feet or hands. Rattlesnakes are found at altitudes up to 9,000 feet in southern New Mexico, about the upper limit to angling.

Ticks

Ticks live in the tall grasses at streamside during the spring and early summer. They can transmit at least three diseases. Rocky Mountain spotted fever is a serious disease, whose symptoms are high fever, flu-like aches, and a red rash. Colorado tick fever is less severe but also causes flu-like symptoms. Lyme disease is another possibility. Its symptoms include fever, headache, stiff neck, a "bulls eye" rash, and extreme fatigue. Later, tingling and numbness, irregular heartbeat, visual disturbances, and seizures may appear. To avoid ticks, cover as much skin as possible with clothing and use insect repellent. Check for ticks at the end of each day. Use the buddy system to check your back and hair. Remove a tick by grasping its head as close to the skin as possible with tweezers, pulling straight out. Avoid putting pressure on the body of the tick to keep from forcing blood back into the skin. Make sure its head is completely removed, then wash and disinfect.

Plague and Hantavirus

Each year several cases of plague are reported from New Mexico. Plague is transmitted by fleas living on host animals. Hantavirus can also be contracted from deer mice. Avoid handling wild animals, particularly squirrels, gophers, and other rodents. Try to keep pets away from wildlife, too, and be sure they wear a flea collar or powder.

Poison Ivy and Hemlock

Poison ivy is common along many streams in southern New Mexico, especially in the Gila National Forest. If you are sensitive to poison ivy use extreme caution when fishing these areas. If you come in contact with poison ivy, wash yourself thoroughly. For normal outbreaks apply calamine lotion or hydrocortisone cream and also take antihistamine or aspirin. Don't scratch because it may cause your rash to become infected. Poison hemlock or water hemlock, poisonous if eaten, has made campers in the Gila very sick. Don't eat any riparian plants, even if they look like garden vegetables.

Horses

Packing into wilderness areas with horses or mules can provide more time to fish. Many of the trails in the Gila Wilderness are in rugged country and some are unsuited to pack stock. Outfitters should be experienced and have stock that are used to the mountains and the narrow, rocky trails. Avoid bringing horses from lower-elevation plains to ride on steep mountain trails. The steep drop-offs and rocky stream crossings can be potentially dangerous when either the horse or rider is a novice.

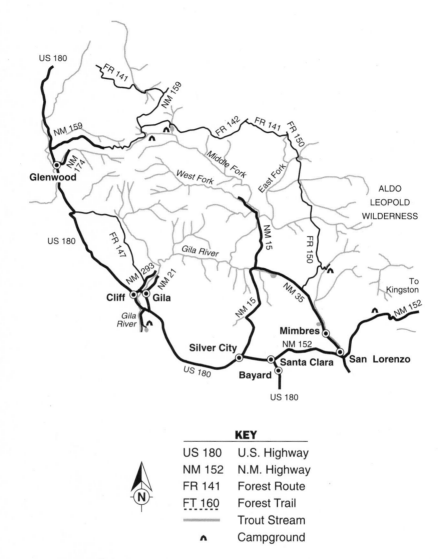

US 180

FR 141

NM 159

NM 159

FR 142   FR 141   FR 150

NM 174

Glenwood

ALDO
LEOPOLD
WILDERNESS

West Fork

Middle Fork

East Fork

US 180

FR 147

Gila River

NM 15

FR 150

NM 293

NM 21

To
Kingston

Cliff   **Gila**

NM 35

Gila
River

NM 15

NM 152

Mimbres

Silver City

NM 152

San Lorenzo

US 180

Santa Clara

Bayard

US 180

KEY

US 180	U.S. Highway
NM 152	N.M. Highway
FR 141	Forest Route
FT 160	Forest Trail
	Trout Stream
∧	Campground

N

Gila National Forest, Gila Wilderness and Aldo Leopold Wilderness

Part II:
Fly-Fishing the Gila National Forest

Gila River emerging from the Gila Wilderness, Watson Mountain

CHAPTER FOUR

Gila River

Gila Mainstem

Location: Gila National Forest, Grant and Catron Counties

Maps: Gila NF Visitors Map; Mogollon Mountains title, USGS 1:100,000 series; USFS Gila Wilderness map

Elevation: 4,700–5,600 feet

Length: 45 miles (Forks to Mogollon Creek)

Best Times: April–November

Fish Species: Sonoran sucker, desert sucker, roundtail chub, smallmouth bass, rainbow trout, brown trout (rare), loach minnow, flathead catfish, channel catfish, green sunfish, carp, spikedace

All the waters of the Mogollon Mountains drain into either the San Francisco or Gila River. The Gila is the larger of the two. It never dries up in New Mexico, where it is a small, wadable, green-colored stream with occasional rapids or cliff-face swimming holes. Its uppermost reach is through a deep, serpentine canyon forced between two mountain ranges—the steeply eroded and rugged Diablos and the elongated, east-west trending Pinos Altos Range. The river cuts south through the Diablos in a narrow defile called Murtock's Hole, then makes a peculiar right turn as it runs into the Pinos Altos at the mouth of Sapillo Creek. From here it flows west until it leaves the big mountains at the mouth of Mogollon Creek—nearly 50 miles of canyon, 40 of it through the Gila Wilderness.

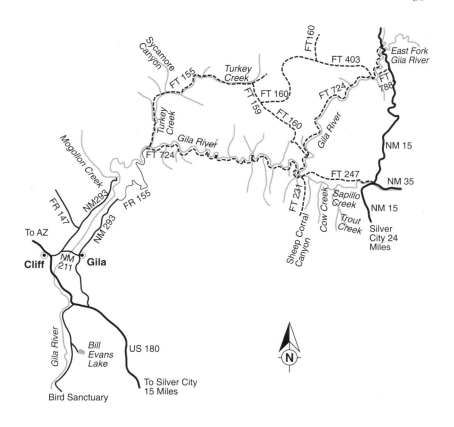

Main Stem Gila River

All told, not many people get into the canyon; most of Silver City's lifelong residents and recent arrivals have glimpsed portions of the river from time to time—after all, it is only 15 to 20 miles away—but few have ever really seen it. Yet the view from above the lower end of the box canyon is not easily forgotten. If you climb over the first ridge on the Turkey Creek Road, you can see a maze of canyon walls, castellated mesas, mountains cut in half, shining green timber far above colored layers of ancient lava flows, and immediately below you, an increasingly lush desert river flowing in mountain shade at the bottom—this is what a wilderness canyon is supposed to look like.

Once the Gila enters the upper box canyon, there are few ways to get to it. For the lower river, follow NM 293, 7 miles north of Cliff; for the Turkey Creek area, follow NM 153 north of Gila to rough, low-standard Forest Road 155 (Turkey Creek Road, subject to wash-outs), thence 12 miles over steep grades to the river. For Gila Wilderness and box canyon reaches, take NM 15 (Cliff Dwellings Highway) north of Silver City. At Sapillo Creek Crossing (junction of NM 15 and NM 35) roughly 20 miles north of Silver City, there is a trail (FT 247) that leads west along Sapillo Creek, then climbs above, 6 miles to the middle portion of the river. For upstream access, take NM 15, 35 miles north of Silver City, where the Alum Trail (FT 785) leads down from an overlook/trailhead 1.25 miles to the river. Two miles farther north, the road itself climbs down to cross the river at the Grapevine Campground Bridge.

Even today, if you hike the box, you can almost count on not seeing anyone else for five to eight days, and if you want to travel this path, be prepared to get wet. Trails have been rebuilt along the river over the years, but floods have obliterated most of the river crossings and many of the benches. The lower section of the box sees many complete sweeping bends, about one every mile or two, which means that you have to cross the river from inside bend to inside bend, as the water rushes along vertical rock walls—a lot of wading, all told. I often bring two pairs of rugged wading sandals, one pair to use, the other to save. In the summer, your nylon shorts will dry out in a matter of minutes under the blazing sun. In winter, find other places to hike.

During March and April the Gila is usually ripping along and adobe colored, a good time for rafting through the box canyon, but not much fun for trout fishing. Heavy summer rains can also turn the river brown for a few days. Most telling of all, summertime water temperatures range from 68–70 degrees at dawn to 76–79 degrees in the heat of the day. Trout cannot survive in water much warmer than this.

Accordingly, trout fishing on the Gila mainstem is rare. Few try, and those who do fish with bait for planted rainbows. Stocking occurs at three places: the Grapevine Bridge on the Cliff Dwellings Highway, the end of Forest Road 155 below the mouth of Turkey Creek, and off the bridges near the towns of Gila and Cliff. The rest of the river is virtually ignored.

Yet for those who fish the river with 9-foot fly rod, 3-weight line, and selected nymphs, this is a very fortunate arrangement. Although trout account for fewer than 1 percent of the river's fish, these few are concentrated in a very small percentage of the water, waiting to be found, and you can catch them fairly regularly from mid-May—or, following a dry winter, from early or mid-April—well into November. Most hiking trips bring at least one wild, stream-reared rainbow or hybrid of 17 inches, and I've seen much larger ones. So few people walk and fish here that I often see my own exclusive accumulation of month-old or older footprints on the sandy banks when I fish in the fall, after summer rains have passed.

Midge and *Baetis* hatches continue on after the summer, and trout rise occasionally even into December, more so than in summer months, when you seldom see a trout rise for anything. During summer I see roundtail chubs and abundant bass rising for mayflies (something the bass aren't supposed to do) as often as the trout. If you insist, as the British are said to do, upon waiting for rising fish and a good hatch (most of the measurable hatches are evening caddis), you'll have a long wait. In fact, you'll wait all summer and most of the fall, like as not. Indeed, I have never seen a really heavy, manna-like hatch on the Gila River.

Yet the stream abounds in insect life. Turn over a large submerged stone anywhere in the river in the summer and you are likely to see it swarming with squat *Heptageniidae* mayfly nymphs of various shades of black, olive, and brown. Look into a still pool and you will see the bottom alive with moving crayfish up to 5 inches long. Roll a large rock in heavy current and you'll often see two or three or more dislodged dobsonfly larvae up to 4 inches float past. Turn a boulder on an exposed mud flat or bank and you will see the abundant pupae of the same insect. Sift through loose underwater sand bars with your hands, and you can find dozens of buried dragonfly nymphs. Though the temperature of the river is unnaturally elevated, the food here, at least, is of blue-ribbon quality. Whenever you do find a trout, rest assured that it is well fed and growing rapidly, as it tries to stake out its territory at the bottom of a choice pool.

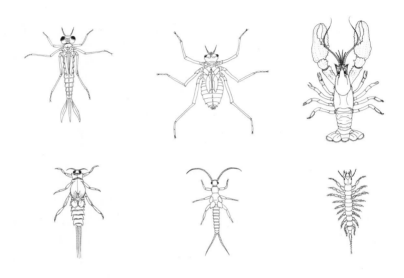

Aquatic Insects. Clockwise from upper left: Damselfly; dragonfly; crayfish; dobsonfly; stonefly; mayfly.

These big, plump trout can be fussy feeders during the summer and fall months. The dobsonflies, "hellgrammites," in particular, seem to be such a favorite food of trout that dark-colored, long-tailed Woolly Bugger fly patterns of sizes 8 to 10, fished right off the bottom, come close to being a secret weapon for them. More than once I have seen well-fed Gila mainstem rainbows refuse to take anything else.

While fishing for trout I have caught plenty of the Gila's many small-mouth bass. In the early 1980s, several articles in the "hook and bul-let press" touted the mainstem as the "best bass river in the Southwest" (which it certainly is not, lagging behind Arizona's Black River). As a result, a considerable number of fishermen showed up in Silver City asking for directions, and, after finding they had to hike and wade to get at the bass, most lost interest immediately.

Occasionally a hot or especially dry summer will decimate the trout in the lower end of the box below Turkey Creek. The summer of 1994 saw most if not all of them wiped out below Mogollon Creek, a few miles below. Yet most years you can expect to catch rainbows, if not browns, all the way from the East Fork to the lush, cottonwood-filled Nature Conservancy preserves just upstream from the forest boundary in the vicinity of Mogollon Creek, even in the hottest part of June. Fish will range from 10 to 16 inches, and their average size is almost exactly the same as that of the Gila trout of a century ago in this same water, a shade less than 12 inches. You won't average one per minute, however, as the pioneers did. Most often, you'll be lucky to hook four or five in a day, as you fish the half-hour before dusk or the hour after dawn in the warm months. The basic limitation is in the number of fish to be found, or more precisely the number of spots in the river capable of supporting trout when the water warms.

Thus, finding the right place to fish is the whole secret. To survive the high temperatures of a summer afternoon, the trout need rapids or other heavy water dropping immediately into a deep pool, preferably one with some shade-producing structure, such as an undercut cliff face or overhanging sycamore tree. Only such conditions provide enough oxygen for trout to survive high afternoon temperatures that make today's river perhaps 5 to 10 degrees warmer than in the last century, when trout were the principal species here. People who frequent favorite swimming holes in the Gila River will often tell you that in the deeper pools there is a surprising cold layer a few feet to a few inches off the bottom. It is in such protected pockets as these, heavily oxygenated by a rapids or series of rapids above, that trout can remain in relative comfort and from which they are very reluctant to stray on summer days. This is where you place your weighted nymph.

You will find them under the rapids and right on the bottom all summer long; in fact, if you fish the pools described above and don't reach the bottom, you may never get to see a trout. You also will come to understand the scarcity of rises on the Gila River.

Saving these fish takes particular care. Sometimes a trout caught and released in the river in summertime will be barely able to muster the strength to swim down to the cooler, better-oxygenated water at the bottom of the pool just a few feet away.

East Fork of the Gila River

Location: Gila National Forest, Grant and Catron Counties
Maps: Gila NF Visitors Map; Gila Wilderness Trail Map; Mogollon Mountains and Truth or Consequences titles, USGS 1:100,000 series
Elevation: 5,600–6,700 feet
Length: 25 miles
Best Times: April–November
Fish Species: Sonoran sucker, roundtail chub, smallmouth bass, rainbow trout, brown trout (rare), loach minnow
Fishable Tributaries: Taylor, Hoyt, Beaver, Diamond, Main Diamond and South Diamond Creeks; Black Canyon and its following tributaries: Apache and Squaw Creeks; Bonner, Aspen, and Falls Canyons

Although it has the largest drainage and provides the most flow, the lowest of the three forks of the Gila, the East Fork, is in the worst condition with the least fishing. Its upper reaches follow a level, partly open valley. Passing through the Gila Wilderness, it narrows progressively in its lower course, joining with the other branches to form the Gila River just beneath the highway bridge at Grapevine Campground. A heavy chain guards a particularly large grapevine above the bank. This vine is older than the neighboring trees, and is nearly all that remains of what was once a dense tanglewood forest arching over the water. The East Fork has plenty of water (25–35 cfs in the summer at the campground) and is 20 to 30 feet wide, with 1-foot riffles and occasional pools running 4 to 5 feet deep. In the upper valley it is a series of shallow runs interrupted by small, sand-filled pools.

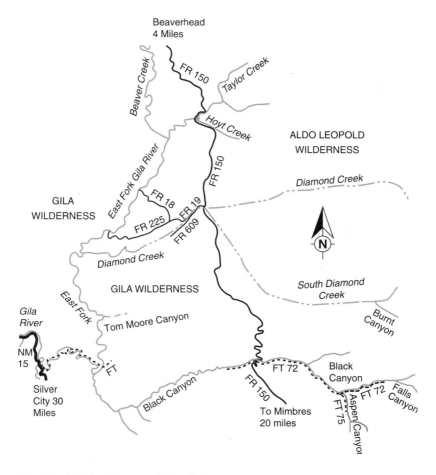

East Fork Gila River and Black Canyon

In summer, the East Fork is 5 degrees or so warmer than the Middle and West Forks and is usually murky. It is easy to note difference in color between it and the cleaner Gila River as the two join beneath the Grapevine Campground Bridge. Here June water temperature in the lower East Fork can soar above 80 degrees, warmer than most heated swimming pools. Temperatures are even warmer in the 18-mile reach above Black Canyon, the East Fork's large, cold, lower-end tributary. One notable feature of the upper river is an almost complete lack of trees. In fact, there is little streamside vegetation of any sort in this area, allowing the direct rays of the summer sun to warm the water. What is more, Beaver Creek, a major upper tributary, is formed by a 75-degree warm spring; and the other tributary, Taylor Creek, is also warmed by the impoundment at Wall Lake.

Intensely grazed benchlands surrounding the river do little to inhibit muddy runoff during heavy summer rains. As a result, mayfly populations show the absence of a number of key indicator species, and caddisfly populations predominate—another sign of impaired aquatic habitats that are unsuited to trout.

Yet rainbow trout are able to survive throughout the East Fork, though numbers are limited in the upper river. You will also find a few browns and many bass of up to 3 pounds.

With its low gradient and high water temperatures in summer, you need to fish the East Fork as though it were a miniature version of the lower Gila, say in the vicinity of Turkey Creek. Expect to find occasional waist-deep pools every 100 or 200 yards. During summer and fall, look for the heavier rapids falling off into the deepest pools in early morning or evening. Scattered sections of the upper reaches (such as the 2-mile reach above Tom Moore Canyon) are fair fishing in the fall, especially in late September and early October. Sometimes results are even better in late spring after the melt waters have cleared somewhat (usually mid-April to early May).

Spring fishing slows, however, as the days get hot. Summer fishing brings another set of challenges. The East Fork gets quite murky and much harder to fish during the summer monsoons. Still, you can pick rainbow trout out of holes between thunderstorms, and there are sporadic Blue Quill, Iron Blue Dun or Blue-winged Olive *Baetis* as well as Hendrickson *(Ephemerella)* hatches that occasionally bring rises. I've caught summer trout on hopper patterns here after sunset.

By far the best section of the East Fork, where the great majority of trout in the stream are to be caught, is the lowest 6 miles below the mouth of Black Canyon. This section has received rest from grazing since 1983, and the changes I have noted since 1987 have been phenomenal.

When I first fished here years ago, I found a typical bombed-out, unproductive Gila Forest stream. A dirt road, since closed by court order, threaded the canyon through sand, weeds, and a few old gnarled cottonwoods. The water was shallow, sandy, and empty, good for a stray trout or two in the course of a morning's fishing. Grass and young trees were just barely starting to show through.

Ten years later, it is hard for me to visualize that nearly lifeless river of 1987. Today the streambank is toed in with dense sedges, knotgrass, and native clover—these seem to be pioneers in the recovery of area streams. Alders, willows, and cottonwoods are also reemerging, providing an intermediate canopy resulting in cool shade over the water's surface for much of the day. The stream is quickly narrowing also, as can be seen by the old alder trees lining the former banks on each side and left stranded away from the water's edge. The runs are deeper. Cattails have helped form miniature marshes where springs pour into the stream below dikes of matted vegetation.

Equally important, accumulating leaf litter can be seen on the bottoms of the quieter pools and riffles, providing food for stream fauna. This section has mayfly populations not found farther upstream, and the largest stream-born insects, the dragonfly, stonefly, and dobsonfly, can be found here. Their imitations bring strikes from the large trout now found in nearly every pool.

You have to reach the bottom with your nymph, just as you must when you fish the Gila mainstem below. I use #10–12 Yellow Stonefly patterns complete with split shot to suggest the *Isoperla* nymphs found in the lower stream. Olive, black, or blue Woolly Bugger patterns of the same size make a passable imitation of the big dobsonfly larvae found in abundance nearly everywhere in the lower Gila forks and mainstem.

The East Fork canyon narrows considerably in this stretch, providing small rapids and deep holes that hold rainbows and hybrids of up to 18 inches. Oddly enough, I have never caught a bass in the river between Black Canyon and the private property boundary above Lyons Lodge, a well-preserved adobe hunting headquarters built behind a hot springs by cattle baron Tom Lyons a hundred years ago. You'll need permission from the owner to fish the private stretch of river surrounding the lodge.

The East Fork has very little developed access; you must walk. The reach below Black Canyon has the highest use; a gated jeep road leads upstream 3 miles from Grapevine Campground (on NM 15, 37 miles north of Silver City), ending at Lyon's Lodge, whereupon a faint streamside trail continues on to the mouth of Black Canyon. There are two blocks of private land here, and at least one landowner requires written permission or other advance notice. The alternative is to climb around the private land (which few attempt), or to scramble down the little-used Military Trail (FT 709), which descends from the base of Buck Hannen Mountain, near the Clinton Anderson Overlook on NM 15. The climb out on this trail involves a 1,500-foot elevation gain, warm and sunny—three water bottles' worth. Upper East Fork has no trail but is accessible in a variety of ways from the sometimes graded but usually rough North Star Road (FR 150), leading from NM 35 north of Mimbres to Beaverhead. Middle access is via the Tom Moore Trail (FT 708), 14 miles west through the Gila Wilderness from FR 150, 2 miles south of Me-Own airstrip/fire base, in the middle of nowhere. Upper East Fork is accessible from FR 150 at Diamond Creek crossing. Take Forest Road 225 to the west, bearing right twice to find FR 18, 6 miles to the river at the old Trail's End Lodge. The other route, one right and one left turn, keeps you on 225 to the Diamond Bar Ranch. These ranch roads seldom see a tourist. Finally, you can find the East Fork at its source by walking 3 miles downstream along Taylor Creek from Wall Lake, also on Forest Road 150, 6 miles south of Beaverhead.

Beaver Creek

Beaver Creek begins as a dry arroyo following the base of 9,400-foot Black Mountain and is brought to life within a narrow, 600-foot box by the very large warm spring on private land. It then flows for 6 miles before joining with Taylor Creek to form the East Fork. Few people realize that fish are in this particular canyon, so similar is it to the many others in Gila country that have no water. Yet Beaver Creek flows for 6 wild, trail-less miles, a verdant green ribbon of canyon bottom pierced by a narrow thread of brown and saffron-gold water. Fishermen of any kind are extremely rare, although cattle enjoy the stream's amenities.

The year-round warmth of the waters below the spring provides for untold leopard and bull frogs in summer, leaping into the water in such numbers as you move upstream that fishing is compromised. There are still sections of wet meadows here—a miracle, considering the heavy grazing. The water's edge is lined with succulent, closely cropped, continuously growing sedges. There is very little tree canopy other than an occasional gnarled and hedged willow or 50-foot cottonwood.

Beaver Creek's upper reaches below the spring contain no trout, but very many bass up to 2 pounds. Some of these seem to have outgrown the water; others of even greater size can be found in a rare beaver pond or two. Sometimes you have to help a hooked lunker continue its battle in the little stream by lifting the stones where it hides, then guiding it to a nearby pool where it can be properly played. A few rainbow trout can be found in this stream near its mouth at the East Fork and along its lower reaches. The stream actually cools as it flows downstream, even in summer, a result of evaporation and streamside seeps.

Taylor Creek

The other branch of the East Fork, Taylor Creek, heads in an impressive canyon system, but has no flow there. Immediately above Wall Lake are a number of cold springs that convert a mere spot of water into a good-sized stream. Thus, Taylor and Beaver constitute two of the Gila Forest's rare spring creeks.

Below the lake, which acts as a summer heat sink, Taylor Creek offers fishing for miniature smallmouths and occasional rainbow trout; sand and muck severely limit spawning activity for the trout. The smallmouths were planted in the East Fork at the Fowler Ranch decades ago with far-ranging results. The fish eventually spread downstream to the Lower Gila Box near the Arizona line, and up the Middle Fork, not to mention the nearby migration up Beaver Creek. They provide fair to good fishing consistently throughout the summer months. Hoyt Creek also empties into Wall Lake and could be recovered for trout. At present it holds miniature bass in a slough in its lower end, on private land.

Black Canyon, Diamond Bar Ranch

Black Canyon

The East Fork's major tributary, Black Canyon is potentially one of the best trout streams in southern New Mexico. The stream is 20 miles long, nearly all within the Gila and Aldo Leopold Wildernesses. It starts just below 10,000-foot Reeds Peak, picks up flow from three tributaries in a high, pine-filled mountain valley, and then flows east to west through a narrow, shady, and, at least partially, black canyon surrounded by piñon-juniper scrub. The lower canyon is not readily accessible to cattle. Black Canyon empties into the East Fork some 3 to 4 meandering miles above Lyons Lodge.

Browns and somewhat fewer Gila hybrids inhabit most of lower Black Canyon below the road crossing, where beaver dams occasionally provide habitat for truly large fish. Gila hybrids predominate above the road. Both species, however, can be found along the entire length of the stream. Fifteen- to twenty-inch browns lurk in some of the pools of the clear, spring-enhanced lower portion of the canyon—fish that are hard to catch during the day in the clear water.

Fire-caused floods blew out Black Canyon and lower East Fork in the summer of 1995, but trout are already starting to return. As of December 1996, the entire watershed is slated to be protected from grazing, and this stream now promises to become a major fishing destination within the Gila Forest. There are also tentative plans to re-introduce Gila trout into upper Black Canyon.

Black Canyon is bisected at its midpoint by the primitive North Star Road (FR 150)—rough but passable in a medium-clearance passenger car—15 miles south of Wall Lake and 20 miles north of its turnoff from NM 35, north of Mimbres. There is an unimproved Gila Forest campground at this spot. A trail (FT 72) leads from the road crossing all the way to the head of the stream. The trail downstream from this same crossing (FT 72) peters out after 2 miles, where the going gets rough. The lowest section of Black Canyon is mostly trail-less and accessible only upstream from its juncture with the East Fork (see East Fork access above). Here tributaries Apache and Squaw Creeks provide limited trout fishing, Apache for browns and Squaw for Gila hybrids.

Aspen, Buckhead, and Falls Canyons

Aspen and Buckhead Canyons, two upper Black Canyon tributaries, drain 9,600-foot Aspen Mountain on the crest of the Black Range; they flow from 7,500 to 8,000 feet and offer a combined total of 3 to 4 miles of habitat. Aspen is tiny, its tributary Buckhead tinier; yet both hold trout and have the potential to provide for many more. Aspen's channel is deeply incised and 3 to 8 feet deep, filled with a few inches of moving water. The low-volume, spring-fed flow is able to support wild browns and Gila hybrids in truly surprising numbers, although I've never seen fish here larger than 8 or 9 inches.

In low water on sunny summer days, these are two of the hardest streams to fish anywhere. There is little if any detectable flow through the major pools, which are perhaps 12 to 16 inches deep and still as glass. Not a shrub, living twig, or follicle hides your approach—just cobblestone and sand bottom, and bare incised banks, with scattered ponderosa pines above the cuts. You can't fish these pools from above the high bank, and you can't wade from below. Between pools is a soundless trickle of water supporting mainly the fishlike *Baetis* mayfly nymphs. The only instream cover is an occasional undercut and uprooted pine that has toppled into the streambed. How the fish manage to survive the bobcats, raccoons, herons, and other predators is a brain teaser.

A fine tippet landing anywhere in one of the pools will put the fish into a panic. Round and round they scurry, clouding the water, not to be seen for fifteen minutes as it slowly clears. As in other tiny streams of the Gila, dry flies work better here simply because they alarm the fish less. In mid-June heat, I can approach fifty or more trout before managing to get one to inspect my tiny *Baetis* imitation.

You can expect better conditions in Falls Canyon, Black Canyon's steepest, uppermost tributary. Here the wild browns and hybrids find better hiding places in the deeper pools, similar to Black Canyon Box in the Black Canyon main branch.

Access to the mouths of all of the upper Black Canyon tributaries is by Forest Trail 72 in the Aldo Leopold Wilderness—off the rough North Star Road (FR 150) and above the old Diamond Bar ranch house. This trail ascends Black Canyon, and Bonner Canyon is the first tributary to appear, 2 miles above the trailhead. Aspen is 6 miles up. Here FT 75 branches off to FT 72, which follows Aspen to its head, passing the mouth of the tiny Buckhead Canyon, 2 miles above. Both streams were depopulated by the 1995 fire.

Diamond Creek System

The middle tributary of the East Fork is Diamond Creek (called Main Diamond Creek in its upper reaches). At 70,000 acres it is one of the larger drainages in the upper Gila system. Diamond Creek flows into the East Fork at that stream's midpoint, and is permanent for 2 miles or so above its mouth. Its middle reaches are dry.

This part of the stream is sad to behold. Although it is too warm and turbid for trout, bass, suckers, cyprinids, and shame-faced cattle have lived in the murky water for decades. Close to a ranch homesite, lower Diamond is a messy Forest Service "sacrifice zone." Current plans are to fence off the entirety of this lower end of Diamond Creek to restore habitat for species like the Southwestern willow flycatcher. If that happens, trout could return.

Above the North Star Road crossing, Diamond Creek accepts several subdrainages—Dry Diamond, Main Diamond, Middle Diamond, East Diamond, and South Diamond Creeks. At least four of these subdrainages were permanent and contained populations of wild Gila trout as recently as 1938—they were even recommended for fishing in *New Mexico Magazine* in that year—but today only the upper end of Main Diamond and a few isolated reaches of the others retain permanent flow. Accordingly, few Gila trout remain, and these have been maintained in the last four years only with continual assistance from the Gila Trout Recovery Team.

The most famous of these substreams, one known to trout experts all over the country, is Main Diamond Creek. It is dry for most of its length; only the upper stream holds reliable water, in a steep-walled, isolated valley.

This glade among the pines was where Robert Rush Miller was sent to find the native trout of the headwaters of the Gila River in 1939 at the old James Brothers Cabin at 7,800 feet in the heart of the remote Black Range, one of the least visited mountain ranges in the continental United States. As reported by Miller, the west-flowing stream was very small, 1.5 feet deep and 9 feet wide, but permanent and presumably trout-bearing from 1.5 miles below the cabin to 7 miles above it (which would be from 7,600 feet to the stream's very head at 9,000 feet, just below Diamond Peak).

The fish in the upper section were much smaller than the native trout originally reported from most other Gila area streams—8 inches and less. Miller was also told that the stream was dry from 1.5 to about 4 miles below the cabin, at which point it became permanent again. In this lower section, which Miller never visited, the largest fish in the stream (12 inches or so) were said to be found among a sequence of "pools" (presumably beaver ponds) in the vicinity of Running Water Canyon. Below these ponds the stream continued to flow for an undetermined length before drying up again. It was generally dry at the crossing of the North Star Road, then came to life again about 2 miles above its junction with the East Fork.

Upper Main Diamond Creek, as Miller saw it, remained virtually unchanged for the next fifty years. As part of the South Fork Grazing Allotment, it had certainly seen its share of cattle. Its banks were grassy and open, the water directly shaded here and there by a few "water birch" (narrow-leaf Arizona alders), or a clump of willows. Arguably one of the most significant trout habitats in the world, this stream for decades held most of the total surviving population of accepted pure-strain Gila trout. State Game Warden Elliot Barker had closed it to stocking of other trout several years before Miller's visit.

Perhaps the fact that trout were still living in Main Diamond, poor as it was, had encouraged forest rangers and game wardens to leave the management of the stream unchanged for many years. Indeed, populations in the upper reach of Main Diamond Creek had varied from five thousand to ten thousand trout one year of age and above. As Miller noted, sizes had been small in this stretch since the 1930s, and the fish were long considered to be overabundant and stunted. Some believed this was due to a higher than optimum pool-to-riffle ratio, stemming from the many check dams and current concentrators built by the Civilian Conservation Corps in the 1930s. Others thought the fish had been underharvested by fishermen.

The Divide Fire of the summer of 1989 came after a record dry fall and winter, during the period of heavy "dry" lightning that often precedes the summer rainy season for weeks. The flames spread north and west, east, almost into Main Diamond Creek at the James Brothers site. About 20,000 acres burned before the fire was quenched by a heavy downpour that carried hail as well as rain. Not only did the downpour put out the fire, it also washed considerable tonnage of ash directly into the stream.

Here the crucial mistake of never having placed many Gila trout into another well-suited habitat quickly became apparent to all. Within one week virtually all the population from the species' mother lode in Main Diamond were dead (only one was found alive in the creek a few days after). A good deal more than half the world's supply of the rarest trout species had suddenly ceased to exist. A new shipment of Gila trout from McKnight Canyon, some three hundred, was returned to the stream in the summer of 1994, ready to make a fresh try. For years trout had been taken from Main Diamond and put into McKnight; now the theme was reversed. In June 1995, the lower permanent reach of Main Diamond Creek near Running Water Canyon was closed permanently to cattle— sort of. The last time I checked they were still there—probably still are.

The Gila trout in Main Diamond are so easy to catch that fisheries biologists have used angling to collect specimens. The feeding habits observed in these fish are typical for most high-elevation streams in the Mogollons containing Gila-type or hybridized rainbow trout. In warm months the fish feed during midmorning and early afternoon. Their chief prey in winter consists of *Chironomidae* and other midge larvae, and feeding is generally confined to the warmest part of the afternoon. When the water warms in late April and early May they tend to select the early emerging mayflies of the genus *Paraleptophlebia* (in this case a generic size 16 Blue Quill).

By early summer the trout become basically omnivorous, feeding in late morning and early afternoon. During this time repeated #16 Blue-winged Olive hatches of the genus *Baetis* occur, but the fish feed on all species and life stages of the stream insects. Finally, after the sum-mer monsoon season has long passed and the willows start to shed their leaves in October, the trout turn their attention to the very abun-dant caddis larvae on the bed of the stream, as well as grasshoppers, beetles, and other terrestrial insects which might fall into the water.

The part of Main Diamond Creek that still flows year-round is hard to find. You start on primitive Forest Road 226 from the Cuchillo-Beaverhead Highway (NM 59) to Lookout Mountain, turning on Forest

Road 500 after 12 miles, following this to the road's end near the head of Turkey Run. Finally, clearing a low ridge via pack trail (FT 42), you descend into the same cool glade that R. R. Miller saw in 1939, where a sparkling trout stream sweeps through stands of yellow pine and Douglas fir. There is an even harder way to get here—15 miles by trail (FT 40) from the North Star Road (FR 150) at the Diamond Creek Crossing.

South Diamond Creek is another disappearing Gila trout stream, in recent years supporting only a handful in roughly 2 miles or less of remaining permanent water. In the early 1990s its population dropped to eighty fish or less, finally dropping to zero in 1995, in spite of yearly reintroductions of 100 to 250 Gilas (already in very scarce supply). In recent years virtually all remaining trout have been found in its tributary, Burnt Canyon—probably one of the smallest trout streams in existence.

Interviews with old-timers conducted in the late 1940s by Fred A. Thompson of the New Mexico Department of Game and Fish indicated that this same stream was once one of the best native trout waters in the region, better, for instance, than the West Fork of Mogollon Creek, which today contains many thousands of trout. Fire in 1995, reminiscent of the one that destroyed the fish in Main Diamond Creek in 1991, provided the final straw. South Diamond Creek is empty as I write. Recovery of the whole Diamond Creek system will take many years.

One last note concerning the East Fork watershed: the National Forest Service currently plans to limit cattle use on virtually the entire East Fork. If this occurs, expect an upstream extension of the good fishing now found below Black Canyon. There are also bigger plans to restore the whole watershed over time, notably the Jordan Mesa and Taylor Creek Grazing Allotments, and to fence off the lower portion of Beaver Creek. Such plans often change, but if all this actually transpires, the upper East Fork area may one day be well worth marking for a visit.

Middle Fork of the Gila River

Middle Fork of the Gila River

Location: Gila Wilderness, Gila National Forest, Catron County

Maps: Gila NF Visitors Map; Gila Wilderness Trail Map; Mogollon Mountains title, USGS 1:100,000 series

Elevation: 5,600–8,000 feet

Length: 43 miles

Best Times: May–October

Fish Species: green sunfish, smallmouth bass, rainbow trout, rainbow-Gila trout, brown trout, Sonoran sucker, longfin dace, loach minnow

Fishable Tributaries: Willow Creek (plus two unnamed tributaries), Turkey, Little Turkey, Gilita, Iron, Snow, Canyon, Clear, Indian, and Prior Creeks; T-Bar, Aspen and Snow Canyons

The Middle Fork of the Gila River heads on the eastern flanks of White-water Baldy Peak and Bearwallow Mountain and is formed where the two streams draining these peaks, Gilita ("little Gila") and Willow Creeks, flow together at about 8,000 feet. Immediately after forming here, the

Middle Fork enters an ever deepening canyon from which it never emerges, flowing for 43 miles before joining with the West Fork a few miles below the Gila Cliff Dwellings National Monument at 5,600 feet. In places the canyon is 1,000 feet deep.

The lower Middle Fork is accessible from the Cliff Dwellings area, via a maze of trails too numerous to mention here. Forest Trail 157 ascends the river directly from a trailhead just north of the Visitors Center parking lot. (If you're up to it, this trail follows the Middle Fork 40-plus miles upstream to its source.) The heavily used Meadows and Jordon Hot Springs Trails (FT 28 and FT 729) cross the river farther upstream. The uppermost portions of the Middle Fork are accessible from the Snow Lake–Beaverhead Road (FR 142), formerly very rough but now negotiable in passenger vehicles during dry weather. Marked trails (FT 705 and FT 706), 4 and 7 miles east of Snow Lake, lead down to the river after a hike of 5 miles or so. There is also a quarter-mile trail leading from Snow Lake Dam down to the river, the shortest access of all. Other, longer trails farther east lead from the same Forest Road 142, down Canyon Creek (FT 71 off spur road FR 917) and above Indian Creek (FT 53 off spur FR 142A). The head of Middle Fork is accessible by streamside trail (FT 157) from Gilita Campground on the Bursum Road (NM 159), 25 miles east of Mogollon. Middle Fork tributaries are accessible by trail within the Gila Wilderness. Consult the Gila Wilderness trail map available from the Forest Service Regional Office in Albuquerque or the supervisor's office in Silver City.

Whereas the Gila River contains an average of about 1 percent trout, the Middle Fork at its mouth contains a somewhat higher percentage, 5 percent or more, which steadily increases to 100 percent in the major headwater Willow Creek. Wild browns, averaging 10 inches but ranging up to 17 inches and occasionally even larger, are the principal quarry in the stream's upper reaches and headwaters, with rainbows starting to show up below Snow Creek and predominating in the lower canyon. Bass, mostly small, and green sunfish have "invaded" the Middle Fork, especially in the lower end. I would classify the Middle Fork as a true trout stream only above 7,000 feet, which is a short way below the mouth of Iron Creek. In its middle and lower reaches, the river is an intermediate warm-water/cold-water fishery, where fishing is slow for occasional good-sized brown and somewhat smaller hybrid rainbow trout.

The most heavily fished large stream in the Mogollons, the Middle Fork has fallen upon hard times lately as a trout fishery. The sections in the vicinity of the Meadows, Jordan, and Big Bear Canyons get worked regularly most of the summer, yet extinct beaver ponds still hold a reserve of good-sized browns, some 15 inches and more. Other sections of the Middle Fork receive only occasional fishing pressure; part of the 8-mile stretch directly above the Gila Visitors Center often seems to be overlooked, as well as the section below Iron Creek, which also provides some of the best results, mainly for browns.

The Meadows should not be a meadows at all. Cattle from the Indian Creek and Jordan Mesa Allotments have traditionally ensured that a grassy meadow did not become a willow forest. Natural clearings along the stream are only marshes and beaver-engineered bogs, both extinct here. The bogs are called *cienegas,* from the Spanish *cien aguas,* or "hundred waters," a reference to their springs.

For many years, it was difficult to travel the Middle Fork without seeing signs of the many cattle which were theoretically not allowed on the stream; yet down they came, through Jordan Canyon, Canyon Creek, and other strategic entry routes. Recently the Forest Service has been cutting back on permitted use on the slopes on the north side of the river within the Gila Wilderness. The results of this are significant in some areas, particularly the stretch between Clear Creek and Canyon Creek, which shows dense new willow and alder growth. Sediments have traditionally washed down into the river from poor-condition ranges bordering the canyon on the north side, affecting redd sites and water quality. Gilita Creek above its junction with Willow provides much silt and warmer, low-quality summer flow, owing both to the 1970s timber activities off Bearwallow Mountain's eastern flanks and to heavy grazing. Snow Creek, formerly a spring-fed stream but now a sometimes warm and soupy outflow from Snow Lake, adds its burden. Perhaps it is as a result of these cumulative factors that the stream has become more desirable for bass and sunfish and less attractive to trout in recent years.

In the 1930s and 1940s, rancher Pete Evans used to amuse visitors by fishing the Middle Fork near the Meadows from the saddle of his horse, catching trout after trout (Gila hybrids) and storing them in his saddle and chaps pockets. Today you need to work the same water very carefully, and you certainly won't need a packhorse to store your catch. The water is particularly dead during the summer heat, for water temperatures will exceed 70 or even 75 degrees during midday in the lower reaches of the stream. When the sun clears the canyon walls in the morning, fishing's over until it drops behind them again toward sunset. Trout can be caught at dawn in most pools, when the water has cooled, and some more browns at dusk.

As the sun weakens in the fall months, the fish continue feeding later in the morning and resume earlier in the afternoon, because water temperatures are now suitably cool for longer periods during the day. Finally, as winter approaches in November and the water changes from warm to cold, the trout become active in the middle of the day, when the water has warmed to ideal temperatures. This process reverses in spring—by early May the trout can be caught in midmorning again.

Willow and Gilita Creeks

Willow Creek has cold, clean water and many fish visible from its banks, even after passing a summer home area and heavily used campgrounds full of enthusiastic trout fishermen. The campground area here offers the best accessible roadside fishing in the Gila Forest. The New Mexico Department of Game and Fish stocks thousands of rainbows here each summer. Not only is it stuffed with wild browns that few seem to catch, but it has two unnamed tributaries at its headwaters within the wilderness boundary, also stuffed with browns.

Farther up yet on both headwaters and in uppermost Willow Creek, the browns peter out and Gila hybrids appear. Willow Creek was proposed as a Gila trout recovery stream in 1994, but political pressure ended the plan.

Fishing in Gilita used to be comparable to Willow Creek—one trout per minute was the reported catch in 1880. Today, the Gilita is turbid, even on sunny late summer and fall days, with a muck and sand bottom completely embedding the natural cobble and volcanic rock substrate. The difference has much to do with the principles of "stump ranching" practiced on nearby Bearwallow Mountain—clearing off timber and then allowing cattle to colonize among the stumps. Old-growth forest in this way becomes a brand new cow pasture, bringing silt to the streambed.

Little Turkey Creek

Little Turkey Creek, another fishable tributary to Willow Creek, empties unnoticed and unfished into Willow right in the middle of the campground development. It is cold and pure, as all streams in the no-graze zone of the Gila Wilderness are, and holds a surprising number of small browns. It even has its own micro-tributary, which occasionally holds fish.

At first glance you will find it hard to believe that trout could live in Little Turkey Creek. Yet there are a half-dozen browns right at the trail crossing whenever I look for them. Apparently they are overlooked by the dozens of hikers who set off from the trailhead at its mouth, many with fishing gear. The browns in these top-elevation tributaries don't have the luxury of hiding out during the daylight hours—they look for food during the day, just like the natives, because of the comparatively limited supply.

When approaching miniature streams like this, it pays to remember that the basic fertility of trout streams in the upper Gila watershed can be two to three times that measured in other parts of the country. In fact, these streams are the most fertile trout waters known, in terms of fish mass per water volume. Native trout streams in the Gila and in northern Mexico can offer as little as .5 cfs of flow and still hide fish of 10 inches or more. "Hide" is an appropriate term here, for there is sufficient food and oxygen but not always ample water for the trout to swim in. Sometimes a fish will have a hiding place and little more in its portion of the stream. Many act like salamanders, slipping under the bank among the roots, heads outward, using the tiny stream itself as a feeding lane. So when you size up a stream like Little Turkey you need to conjure up an image of some other stream in the cold country two or three times its size.

Iron Creek

After the waters of Gilita and Willow Creek meet, the Middle Fork turns into an intermediate- to good-quality brown trout fishery for 10 miles or so before meeting its best tributary, and one of the best streams in the region, Iron Creek. This drains northeastward from 10,900-foot Whitewater Baldy and 10,500-foot Center Baldy in the high Mogollons and flows for 11 miles through the wilderness from 8,800 to 7,100 feet before joining the Middle Fork as its only major tributary. The best fishing in Iron Creek is in the lower end below the trail crossing (FT 151). The upper reaches are small and gravelly.

Water quality in Iron Creek is superb. The middle and lower reaches have good-quality stream cover, consisting of a variety of willow species, Arizona alder, box elder, plus an occasional growth of narrowleaf cottonwood, with active beaver colonies in the lower stream. Higher up on the mountain, the streambed is less stable, with higher-elevation redstem dogwood, forbs, and grasses in open glades bounded by white and Douglas fir. The uppermost stream is filled with downed trees for much of its length. Stoneflies are unusually abundant in the cold water (many streams in the Gila don't have them), comprising up to 10 percent of the aquatic insects.

Browns and a few hybrid rainbows are in the lower end, with browns and, rarely, a stray Gila trout in the middle and upper reaches. You will not see many browns larger than 12 or 13 inches, but if you fish carefully you have the right to expect three good fish in a half-hour or less. Most of these will be 7 to 10 inches. A population of Gilas of up to 10 inches is found in a closed section of the stream above a man-made barrier at 7,700 feet. If by some fluke you ever find a Gila trout on your line in the legally fishable portion of the stream, you must return it to the water immediately.

Owing to the clear water, I've had best success with very small sinking patterns, fished in the standard manner—cast upstream into the heads of shallow riffles or into pockets along undercut banks, then drifting downstream in a 90- to 120-degree arc. In low light the browns move into the shallower water to feed. It's easy to scare a large fish as you move along, looking ahead to the pool where you expect it to be. Also, the browns in Iron Creek don't seem to hole up in the middle of the day, as they do in the larger, warmer streams, and you find a number of smaller fish sharing the same pool, rather than one old cannibal and little else.

In the old days this area was stocked regularly by the Game and Fish packtrain making the rounds over Turkeyfeather Pass between Willow Creek and the West Fork. Today's backpackers use this same wilderness thoroughfare as a pathway to good fishing. Reach Iron Creek from the Forest Trail 151 trailhead just off NM 159 near the Willow Creek Ranger Station. A fairly easy 4-mile hike will get you to the stream.

Canyon Creek

Canyon Creek enters the Middle Fork several miles below Iron Creek. The stream starts on the eastern edge of the T-Bar Grasslands; then, shortly after crossing open country and passing beneath a culvert on Forest Road 142, it enters a narrow canyon where it picks up several springs before flowing southward through the Gila Wilderness. Fishing water begins at the old Hulse ranch house just above the wilderness boundary, and continues below 4 to 5 miles (although the stream occasionally dries for a half-mile or so as it passes through a weedy, open valley once farmed for spring wheat).

Little Gila types inhabit the lower reaches, although rainbows have been planted at the Hulse Ranch for the enjoyment of grandchildren. There are occasional 10-inch trout in this section, easily caught.

Presently the fish in Canyon Creek are a bit too small to bother with, yet the stream is currently being rested from grazing. If the one hundred cattle of the Canyon Creek Allotment don't return to the stream bottom, if the willows continue their comeback, and if beavers from the Middle Fork decide to recolonize in the canyon, this picture could change.

West Fork of the Gila River

Location: Gila Wilderness, Catron County

Maps: Gila NF Visitors Map; Gila Wilderness Trail Map; Mogollon Mountains title, USGS 1:100,000 series

Elevation: 5,600–8,600 feet

Length: 36 miles

Best Times: May–October

Fish Species: Gila-rainbow, rainbow, and brown trout, Sonoran suckers, roundtail chubs, longfin dace

Fishable Tributaries: McKenna (closed to fishing), White, and Cub Creeks; Rawmeat, Langstroth, and Trail Canyons; one unnamed headwater tributary

The West Fork of the Gila River lies almost entirely within the Gila Wilderness. As with the Middle Fork, the easiest access is from the Gila Cliff Dwellings on NM 15, 44 miles north of Silver City. A passable hiking trail (FT 151) follows the river for most of its length before climbing out of the upper canyon at 7,600 feet and ending at Willow Creek Campground, 36 miles away. Willow Creek Campground is just off the Bursum Road (NM 159), 24 miles east of Mogollon. This trail is the most direct way to access the river. The mouths of all but two tributaries of the West Fork (McKenna Creek and the headwater branch) can be reached via the same trail. The West Fork itself starts on the north side of 10,770-foot Mogollon Baldy, running off the West Fork Saddle. It joins the Middle Fork just above the Gila Visitors Center, 2 miles below the Gila Cliff Dwellings, and the flow continues on to the East Fork mouth at Grapevine Bridge.

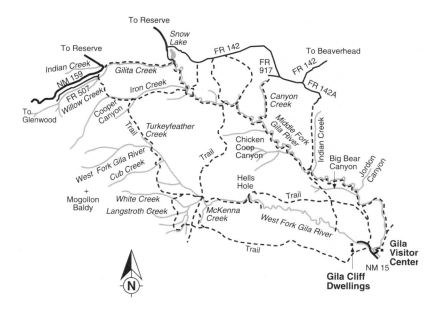

West Fork Gila River and Middle Fork Gila River

Of the Gila River's three forks, this is the steepest and smallest in both area of drainage and water volume; it sometimes runs only intermittently in its lower end above the Visitors Center. Floods hit it hardest, but it is in the best fishing condition. Virtually its entire watershed, in the heart of the Gila Wilderness, has not been grazed by cattle since the middle to late 1960s, some portions longer. Beaver are normally found scattered along the length of the stream, although their numbers seem to have fallen recently. Vegetation is slowly returning along the lower reaches.

Earlier in this century, some area ranchers thought the barren stream-banks of the Gila forks incapable of growing cottonwoods. Yet in the 1880s not only were cottonwood groves present, but trout were so abundant here that cowboys were able to scare fish upstream in great numbers into deep pools where they could dip them onto the banks with their hats. No need for a pole in those early days.

The head of the West Fork is small and unstable, full of loose gravel deposits laid by recurrent floods; flow is small. The most notable feature

of fishing here is the existence of Gila-type trout in the extreme upper
reaches, including one small unnamed tributary entering from the north,
3 to 4 miles above Turkeyfeather Creek. These beautiful little fish are
always of interest.

In the creek-sized upper West Fork, say in the canyon pools below
Turkeyfeather Creek, it is possible to have good cooperation from the
browns (which almost completely dominate the stream here) on dry
flies, a real rarity in the Gila. I sometimes try a Pink Humpy imitation
of the red-colored mayfly of the *Epeorus* genus, the Alberti, or Pink
Albert. The Adams, suggestive both of caddis sedges and flying mayfly
forms, also works in sizes 14–16.

Actually, browns and the other trout species do periodically take
dry flies elsewhere in the Gila. If I were to fish dry flies by habit, as I
did many years ago, I undoubtedly would catch trout regularly in the
summer in all high-elevation waters in the Mogollons; but now I fish
with dry flies only when it offers some advantage. This is generally
when the flow is so low and the water so quiet that a nymph cannot
be cast without frightening the fish, and the fish cannot be approached
closely enough to dap the bait into the water.

Springs and seeps enter the stream from both banks at Turkeyfeather
Creek mouth, swelling the flow where the narrows of the West Fork
begin. It is at this spot that the stream becomes a full-fledged creek,
though fish do indeed range several miles above. Below are many rapids,
falls, and pools of native volcanic traprock in a small canyon. The trout
are almost entirely browns.

The main trail from Willow Creek meets and follows the bottom of
this mini-canyon until reaching Cub Creek, at which point the canyon
gets deeper and the trail climbs onto the ponderosa parklands on the
mesa above. If you decide to forego the trail at this point and follow
the stream down the 3 or 4 miles to White Creek mouth at the Jenks
Cabin, you'll have a first-class trout stream all to yourself. When floods
haven't cleaned them out, the clear pools are chock full of 9- to 12-
inch browns, a few larger. Below White Creek mouth at 7,000 feet, the

West Fork enlarges greatly and changes from a smallish, high-elevation creek to a fair-sized, mid-elevation stream.

An acquaintance once landed a 26-inch brown in the West Fork about a quarter-mile below White Creek (in the 1970s), but a 14-incher is quite respectable today. The West Fork trail climbs away from the bottom here for 2 or 3 miles. It is superb water, a much bigger stream in this trail-less section, with holes close to 20 feet deep and fast water. Rainbows now show up in numbers in this stretch. In fact, most of the catch is rainbows of 9 to 12 inches, and occasionally 14 to 15 inches. The browns tend to be a bit larger, on the average.

People have fished in the vicinity of the Jenks Cabin for a long time. A 21.75-inch Gila trout was caught in the 1930s in this same stretch, between White Creek and McKenna Creek—the largest Gila trout recorded to date. A 1931 report of an informal census conducted here (with spinners used to attract the fish and bring them within view) tallied eight hundred catchable trout in just one half-mile, some of them from 20 to 26 inches—an amazing number of fish from a stream providing 10 to 15 cfs of late summer flow in a good year.

The water warms as the canyon opens up a bit just above the horseshoe bend passing by the mouth of (fishless) Hell's Hole Canyon. Sycamore trees, a signature of a lower-elevation stream, start to appear farther downstream at about 5,900 feet, just above Grave Canyon mouth, where the first roundtail chubs start showing up. Sonoran suckers, too, start to appear a bit farther downstream. Blacktail rattlers grow big here, and they will strike—an old fishing hat of mine used to bear a permanent venom stain on the bill as a reminder of that fact. Smaller horseshoe bends follow continuously in the section below Hell's Hole Canyon, for instance near the mouths of Ring and Nat Straw Canyons, providing moderate-sized pools and consistently good fishing for 9- to 11-inch rainbows, some larger. Browns up to at least 16 inches also show up, though less frequently. The browns hide in the shade during the day, but they will nonetheless take nymphs drifted under deep banks all morning, if they don't have to move too far for them. The rainbows prowl most of the

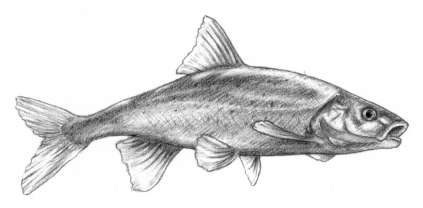

Roundtail Chub

runs and the deeper pools below heavy water, feeding mornings and afternoons in the summer, where occasionally a 15- or 16-inch 'bow will deliver a jolting strike. These are all wild, stream-born fish.

Floods regularly level the stretch from EE Canyon to the Gila Visitors Center, tearing down trees and damaging bridges. Most of it is open, level, sunny, and filled with gravel and sand. Yet this section is the most heavily fished stretch. The lower section between the Middle Fork mouth (just above the Visitors Center) and the Grapevine Campground is slightly better, with rainbows and a few hard-to-fool browns in the larger pools. Beaver occasionally provide pools above and below the mouth of Little Creek, while NMG&F pack-stock use portions of the bottom as a pasture, on the Heart Bar Ranch property purchased by the state forty years ago to provide wildlife habitat.

Fingerlings used to be planted along the 12 miles between the Cliff Dwellings and Hell's Hole Canyon, but the practice ended in 1986. The West Fork is currently stocked no farther upstream than the footbridge at the Gila Cliff Dwellings National Monument. With reduced stockings, fishing pressure has gone down in the lower end of the West Fork in recent years.

The pattern found on the West Fork—rainbows below, predominantly browns in the middle and upper reaches, then Gila hybrids in the headwaters—is common in the Gila River watershed. In the very lowest elevations of many streams what appear to be Gila hybrids sometimes reappear, possibly because they better tolerate the warmer water and periodic floods. Floods always seem to hurt the browns. In general, browns in the Gila watershed are not found much below 5,600 feet. Rainbows and Gila hybrids, by contrast, can be found in surprising quantity at elevations nearly 1,000 feet lower, in smaller streams and, occasionally, larger waters.

Cub Creek

Cub Creek is White Creek's smaller twin, tucked between Cub Mountain and the northern outrider of Mogollon Baldy in its very steep upper reaches and flowing from almost 9,000 to 7,500 feet in its 3 or so miles of fishable water. It flows through a mini-canyon of its own and joins the West Fork canyon where it starts to cut under the Jerky Mountains. At Cub Creek mouth, the West Fork is almost entirely brown trout water, and Cub Creek, also, contains browns plus Gila hybrids, which predominate above. Its upper end holds fish of surprising size but is almost too small for angling. This stream is also slated for eventual Gila trout renovation, as is the whole headwater area of the West Fork.

Fishing is generally so easy in this stream as to hardly require comment. The hybrids feed as though on cue, while only the larger browns hesitate. One peculiarity of Gila hybrids I've noticed over the years is their tendency to pay less attention to nymphs drifted along passively in the current than to the same lures jigged, twitched, or even raced upstream against the current—a sort of "greed reflex," as it were, among these perpetually hungry little fish. This fishing technique is, of course, something that will send brown trout diving for cover. Properly presented flies will bring a sudden, vicious strike from these browns. The Gilas, by contrast, often take very deliberately on a dead drift, while chasing after and socking something seen moving under its own power.

White Creek, Langstroth, Rawmeat, and Trail Canyons

One of the best small streams in the Gila Forest, White Creek was originally named for the milky color of the water as it flowed over slate-green bedrock. This whitish color is common in many streams and smaller rills during high spring meltwater flows. Quite often it is the mark of a drainage that dries up in summer, but White Creek has reliable flow for its entire length. It is crystal clear today, and always cold. The upper part is somewhat smaller, falling off the northeast face of Mogollon Baldy, flowing for 7 to 8 miles in a relatively open little valley way up at the 8,000- to 9,000-foot level before dropping almost straight down into a deep canyon shared with the West Fork. This upper portion of the creek has been reclaimed for Gila trout above a natural barrier a mile and a half above its confluence with the West Fork. It is closed to fishing.

White Creek below the barrier still gets fished regularly at the old Jenks Cabin, which is still used by the Forest Service as a bunkhouse for employees and unofficial guests. Above the cabin the White Creek stream bottom is level and easy to follow before boxing up at the confluence of the other tributaries; the steeper box section offers some good little pools. Below the cabin, on the west side of the creek, are the marshy remains of the old trout-rearing ponds, kept up after all these years by a rare colony of beavers, and fed by an unnamed spring rill. They now hold wild browns instead of hatchery Gilas. The ponds are small but ice-cold and overlooked by fishermen, containing equally overlooked but easily spooked fish, mostly browns. The lower end of White Creek still holds mostly browns, some quite large. Beaver dams form a sequence of ponds at the mouth, where occasional summer-evening hatches attract mainly juvenile trout. I found a fair number of rainbows in the lower mile of the stream.

Below the barrier, White Creek acquires the flows of Rawmeat, Langstroth, and Trail Canyons—three gemlike, rushing streams that are 2, 6, and 2 miles in length, respectively. In their lower sections, these streams flow through nearly identical steep, narrow canyons. All three willow-lined streams offer fast fishing for beautiful 6- to 10-inch (and sometimes a bit larger) Gila hybrids, plus browns of up to 14 inches in the lower reaches. Rawmeat, barren in its steep upper reaches, has a brief section lower down where the moss-covered west wall hangs over the bed of the creek. A line of springs falls from this wall directly into the stream, providing near-constant shade and a perpetual, ice-cold rain, guaranteed to wet your hat and shirt—very welcome in June's heat.

Moving upstream in these plunging, boulder-filled canyons gives you every advantage over the fish waiting inevitably in the golden pools and shaded side-pockets. If you are careful, you can see them and plan your approach long before they see you.

In its upper reaches, Langstroth Canyon's fish are dead ringers for Gila trout, protected from the browns by steep rapids in the narrow lower canyon. This was once the favorite fishing water of Edwin Shelley, Gila trout expert and manager of the Jenks Cabin trout hatchery at the mouth of White Creek in the 1930s. The Gila hybrids in these streams seldom if ever see a fly and are easily caught—when they are feeding, that is. The fish disappear from view when they are not hungry, and are seen everywhere in the stream when they are; midmorning and midafternoon are the meal times during the summer.

A few years ago in upper Langstroth Canyon, I found a 2-inch drag-onfly nymph and out of curiosity tossed it into a knee-deep pool filled with the Gila types (yellow, rosy redband, amber cutthroat markings, etc.). Immediately, one of the fish tried to gulp down the swimming *naiad.* Then I cast a small dry fly into the pool's center, and the dragon-slayer itself rose and hooked into the Adams; by the time I got to remove the hook, the *naiad's* eyes were just visible, protruding from in the fish's gullet. Such is the ease of landing an eager, brightly colored Gila hybrid from the headwater tributaries of the West Fork.

All three of these streams have been slated for eventual Gila trout recovery, yet these (and other) hybrid populations may well contain unique Gila trout genes.

McKenna Creek

McKenna Creek, named after a local homesteader who also inspired a Gregory Peck Western, drains the former open savannah above and around McKenna Park (now rapidly filling in with younger pines). The creek rises from springs as it falls into a mini-canyon a little less than 2 miles above the West Fork, deep in the Gila Wilderness. It flows into the river at about 6,700 feet, forming at its mouth a 6-foot waterfall, high enough to protect the purity of one of five known and accepted relict populations of Gila trout. D. M. Regan reported Gila trout in McKenna Creek in 1964 and 1966, which in 1970 were pronounced pure. Since that time, however, DNA analysis has suggested that the McKenna Creek fish may also contain rainbow trout genes.

The lower quarter-mile of the stream is often filled to the brim with white muck from a side canyon, which also serves as something of a fish barrier. Fish occasionally fall out of the stream during high water and land in the West Fork. This natural restocking of the parent stream has in the past only slightly counteracted the nearby plantings of several thousand rainbow trout fingerlings yearly by the NMG&F.

Little Creek

Little Creek is a small stream that parallels the lower West Fork—rising in the north side of the Diablos in a long, narrow drainage, then emptying the West Fork a little less than a mile above Gila Hot Springs. The size of this drainage compares with Turkey Creek and Mogollon Creek, the other major streams of the Diablo Range, but the stream is intermittent through most of its upper reaches. Six miles or so above the mouth, large cold springs pour out in a curtain of water from a moss-covered rock face and fall into the creek's narrow, shady canyon as it passes below 8,000-foot Brushy Mountain. The only really good fish habitat on Little Creek is within this last 6 miles of the stream.

Earlier in the century, Little Creek and its main tributary, Little Turkey Creek, were noted for their "black-spotted natives," or Gila trout. A big fire on the flanks of Granite Peak in 1951 caused heavy erosion in the middle section of the creek, which now flows only under several feet of accumulated debris. This historic "sea change" is nothing unusual in the Gila; you can expect Little Creek to resume its normal flow in a century or two. Little Creek still has a short permanent reach in the upper headwaters, after which the stream remains intermittent for 10 miles or so. Then, some 3 miles above the Miller Springs Trail Crossing (FT 160) it acquires a very modest flow. Below the crossing, it appears to acquire more subsurface water at the usually dry mouth of Little Turkey Creek, but this is only a mile or so above the stone-and-mortar fish barrier built in 1981 to protect the Gila trout. The placement of this barrier gives a bit of a pause to the thoughtful observer, for about a half-mile below are the big springs which turn Little Creek into a real trout stream, still open to fishing. Gilas are sometimes washed down into the legal waters after heavy rains.

Although only a modest five hundred fish live in the upper stretch of Little Creek, it has one of the largest populations of Gila trout in existence. Ironically, although the Gila trout in this protected reach are mostly in the 5- to 7-inch range, below the big springs you can find browns and occasionally rainbows of much larger size—none of the superb trout habitat provided in the lower stream has been reclaimed for the natives.

The easiest way to fish Little Creek is to start at the bridge on the Cliff Dwellings Highway (NM 15). Many summertime fishermen pass the crossing on their way to and from various degrees of disappointment without giving any thought to the small stream passing beneath the roadway. Ugly-looking riprap has been set in place here by state highway officials worried about flooding.

A bit farther up the stream, the fisherman will see seemingly empty pools, but he will also notice that the water feels several degrees cooler than the Gila River—particularly if he has followed the creek up after inspecting its river mouth first, as I always do. He will also note how narrow and well shaded the stream bottom is, with alders crowding each streambank, and willows and cottonwoods abundant enough to support the beaver, whose cuttings and dams also line the banks. Rushes cover sandbars, and alder branches hang right over the stream.

How many people would guess that every one of these apparently empty pools holds brown trout? I don't know how many fishermen stop here, but I've fished this 6-mile stretch many, many times. It has seldom failed, and I've never met a soul. Yet on any given day you can leave this cool shady retreat, cross the nearby bridge over the Gila River at the forks, and see many hopeful souls sitting on the bank and catching only a good sunburn.

My favorite time to fish Little Creek has always been on fall evenings, when browns prepare to spawn and leaves start to turn. In every large pool is a large fish, and often as not that large fish will dart toward, or seize with deliberation, a traditional Muddler Minnow or modern synthetic mylar-and-fur Zonker, olive or yellow, then try to break it off the line. It is always a shock to see one of these large fish rush out from its hole under the bank to have a look. By the end of your night's fishing, if a particularly large fish hasn't broken your line, then your Zonker will at least have become shredded by sharp teeth.

For years I was very careful about even parking my car within sight of the Little Creek highway sign, for fear that someone would figure out what I was doing there. Now I am telling. Henry David Thoreau, an occasional trout fisherman himself, once said that time is only a stream to go fishing in—and it's been years since I fished Little Creek. I'm still restless, though less sure of what I'm after, and I'm always looking for new things, variations on a very fine theme. I would be happy if someone else could be walking up Little Creek now—or on some October evening, years from now—still finding good fish there. And I would hope that he would look just as carefully, move just as slowly, and feel just as possessive about the place as I once did.

CHAPTER FIVE

Streams Of the Pinos Altos Range

The few beautiful streams flowing into the Gila River off the steep north slope of the Pinos Altos (Tall Pines) Mountains are in the wilderness and hard to reach. Six others drain the same range farther east(lying north and northeast of Silver City)—all easier to find and containing at least some fishing for wild populations of brown or rainbow trout. These other waters are, with one exception, nothing to write home about. They are typical of the neglect visited on many other streams in the Gila Forest. Southwestern New Mexico was better noted for its fishing fifty years ago than it is today because a good portion of the streams that are left have come to resemble the type of water you find right out of the town of Silver City.

Sapillo Creek

Location: Gila Wilderness, Gila National Forest, Grant County
Maps: Gila NF Visitors Map; Mogollon Mountains title, USGS
1:100,000 series
Elevation: 5,200–6,000 feet
Length: 10 miles
Best times: September–November
Fish species: rainbow trout, longfin dace, Sonoran suckers, possibly brown trout
Fishable Tributaries: Sheep Corral, Cow, Trout, and Meadow Creeks

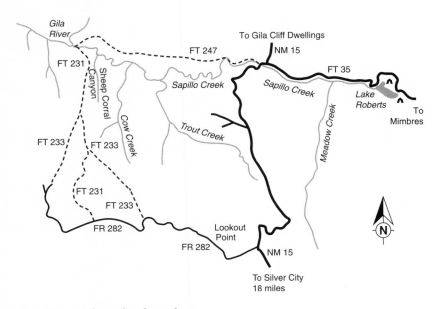

Sapillo Creek and Lake Roberts

Sapillo Creek, the major stream of the Pinos Altos Range, arises in an open valley on the west side of the Continental Divide, passing the old GOS Ranch headquarters north of Mimbres, then picking up its permanent water at 6,000 feet in large springs below Terry Canyon (now welling up onto the bottom of Lake Roberts). Below the Lake Roberts Dam the creek flows west, passing ever-growing, summer-home developments as the valley pinches together. Finally, just below the NM 15 crossing, the stream falls into a narrow, almost subterranean, box canyon for its last winding 6 to 8 miles. It flows into the Gila River at 5,200 feet, in a place where the river makes a sudden 90-degree westward bend.

In recent years the Forest Service has built a hot, up-and-down trail following the rim on the north side of the box, which finally switches down to the Gila River at Sapillo mouth. But this is of little use for fishermen. There remain two other ways to get down to the water. You can hike down to the mouth via the Sheep Corral Trail (FT 231). This starts at the Sheep Corral Road (FR 282), which you follow some

7 miles west of its junction with the Cliff Dwellings Highway (NM 15) near the crest of the Pinos Altos Range. The other way is to begin at Sapillo Crossing and start wading down the creek itself—the way the stream was fished in the 1930s, when it was a fishing stream known to local guides. You still have to scramble and wade, for there is no trail, always keeping an eye on the weather. High flow in the box can mean 10 to 15 feet of extra water.

At one particular spot, where most hikers turn around and head back upstream, and where the cattle absolutely have to turn back, you can touch both canyon walls with your outstretched arms. Soon you must either wade, or swim, down a narrow pool or else crawl through a debris-choked passage through the canyon wall itself. Below this spot, a short way below the mouth of Trout Creek, the streamside vegetation starts to come to life. Passing through this barrier is almost like opening a door and entering a private garden. From this point on, you feel that you are truly in what is left of the wild Gila.

The lower canyon of the Sapillo lies within the Gila Wilderness and still holds trout, but it is so narrow that it is difficult to see from above on either side. As you climb 6 miles down the Sheep Corral Trail (say in June, when it's indescribably bright and hot), dropping off the hazy blue ridges of the Pinos Altos Range, you can place where the Sapillo Box should be, but you can't see it. Only the ochre, bricklike Gila conglomerate is visible above it, hot as an oven, sprinkled with a few hard-pressed juniper trees stretching up to a low ridge. You can't make out the break in the rock marking the slot of the canyon. Later in the day, as you climb back out with the sun low in the sky, you can see a thin black shadow slicing lengthwise across the bedrock, and that will be it.

Only when you are hovering directly over the box, where it pours into the Gila across from the base of a mountain-sized horseshoe bend, can you at last see the pebbly bed and clear water of the Sapillo. Here you descend from what feels like desert to what feels like Michigan. The trail passes through a deeply shaded grove of Rocky Mountain maples, and when you finally touch the canyon bottom you are in nearly complete shade, yet with the stream golden and glowing from light reflected time and again off the canyon walls, its banks lined by dark green alders and brilliant white, fan-leafed sycamores.

It is very dangerous to be in the Sapillo Box during heavy rains. In many places the water has nowhere to go but up. Remember, this is a stream that drains nearly 100,000 acres, and heavy rains can represent 15 percent of the annual precipitation. As any fly fisher can tell you, there is a tremendous difference between wading in rapid current up to your calves and in current up to your waist or chest. I've seen flood-wood perched 20 feet above the canyon bottom.

Practically all the vegetation in Sapillo Canyon, especially leaf litter, falls into and along its streambed. Willow and sycamore leaves are always visible along the bottom. In some sections alder trunks reaching out of the water make a solid instep above the stream. Trees growing on each side send branches out to meet overhead. Wherever you see such plant life, you can be assured that many fish are in the water. There were once brightly spotted half-pound Gila trout and little else in both the river and the creek. If you look carefully into the water you might see fish darting for cover. They are rainbow trout, some from the river, some stream born, and some wanderers. Cattle are not here, for they can't pick their way down very far from Sapillo crossing.

Although it gains several trout-supporting tributaries from the Pinos Altos Range, Sapillo has always been considered to be marginal water because of warm summer flows. Its water is heated and muddied by man, however, not nature. When the valley becomes a summer sun bowl, the stagnant Lake Roberts becomes a heat sink as well. The creek gets hot. Cold springs lie on the bottom of Lake Roberts, but the water leaving the lake is nothing like flow from a spring. During the rainy months of July and August, the ephemeral tributaries draining heavily grazed uplands along the Continental Divide bring a flood of sediment down the valley and into Lake Roberts, which acts as a large silt trap. Between the dam and the Cliff Dwellings Highway crossing 6 miles below, sediments have filled the pools, and erosion has widened the streambed. Below the lake fishing is poor, although stray rainbows can sometimes be found near the dam.

The box canyon begins shortly below the road crossing, and things start to improve here. I've never measured the June water temperatures in the box, but they too must approach 80 degrees at times, forcing the trout into cooler pockets of water, mainly in deep pools and near springs. Somehow they are able to survive. After the water cools in fall you find them throughout the stream, and the trout here can get surprisingly large.

In the 1930s, when the Sapillo Valley was still remote ranch country and the middle reaches used as a pasture, nearly all the trout in the Sapillo were Gila trout and Gila hybrids up to 14 inches or so, migrants from the Gila River. To catch some, you had to follow the creek downstream to a 10-foot waterfall about 5 or 6 miles below the road crossing and a short way above the mouth of Cow Creek and its 20-foot falls. Above the falls were only roundtail chubs. The creation of Lake Roberts in 1965, and the subsequent stocking of many thousands of trout, changed fishing on the Sapillo somewhat. Now the migrants seem to move downstream, not upstream, from the impoundment down the Sapillo and into the Gila River itself. As a result, you are never really sure when you might pick up a 15- or 16-inch rainbow in the Sapillo. Although trout are outnumbered by suckers in this stream by a ratio of ten to one, I have found truly big trout all through the box. The best time seems to be middle to late fall, as late as you care to wade. Feeding behavior of these trout is simple; I seldom see a trout in the box turn an offering down, at least when the water is cool. After you reach the water, move slowly. If you can tell the difference between the Sonoran sucker, which will not take a fly, and the rainbow, which will, then you are in business. You wade next to the wall until you can spot one, then you cast for it. This little box is an echoey, 6-mile tunnel, 200 to 500 feet deep, its bottom filled with water. Don't take your best rod. I've broken two in there (and still caught fish).

Trout Creek

The Cliff Dwellings Highway(NM 15) follows uppermost Trout Creek for a mile or so, crosses it, then, miles beyond, overlooks a 600-foot canyon with the same stream now at the bottom. In recent years water has flowed for only 4 miles at the canyon's lower end, where it empties into Sapillo Creek. The upper reach is a naked arroyo with gravel banks—currently there is not even grass.

You have to go way down to get to where the fish are by wading down Sapillo Creek to meet the stream, or climbing into the canyon. Neither way is easy. The climb is steep, the wade down Sapillo is tough. The more direct way is the climb; then you follow the dry canyon of Trout Creek itself until you reach water. There is a woodcutter's road on Wildhorse Mesa that you can use; it enters NM 15 on the west side just below the unmarked overlook above the canyon. Follow this rough two-track, bearing to the right at the first fork, until you reach a fence and stock tank. Then, down into the canyon you go, taking care not to step on the many agave plants growing on the slopes. If you don't see water when you finally reach the canyon bottom, head downstream. Then, if you don't see trout, do the same. Reliable water is supplied via a side canyon from the west, aptly called West Canyon. Below West Canyon, for about 3.5 miles, the fishing is spotty for wild brown trout before Trout Creek debauches into the Sapillo, trailing algae as it goes.

As with most Gila streams holding wild browns, there are some larger fish persisting from year to year in the choice pools. Browns in the 14-inch range have been taken, though many will die in a drier-than-usual year.

Cow Creek

Names can deceive. Immediately to the west of Trout Creek is a stream called Cow Creek, which, like Trout Creek, flows into the Sapillo: thesis, antithesis. As of 1996, Trout Creek has few trout and many cows, Cow Creek few cows and many trout, as well as Rocky Mountain maple, box elder, peachleaf willows, and Arizona alders. Of all the trout streams near Silver City, this is the only one which is truly pleasurable to walk, wade, or observe, from end to end. There is no trail here, and you must hike cross-country to find the canyon. The closest access is Forest Road 282 (Sheep Corral Road), which intersects NM 15 about 15 miles north of Silver City.

Though far from pristine, Cow Creek is still a good stream to fish. It has more miles of water than Trout Creek, but has not gouged as deep a canyon as its neighbor. Its lower 2 miles are a series of chutes and smaller falls separated by shady cobblestone riffles. Higher up on the mountainside, the stream comes to life at 6,200 feet, where a snaking chute of water etched into the pink bedrock falls 10 to 15 feet into a deep, green pool. Looking down into this pool from the canyon wall, you can see the black shadows of trout moving along the bottom. Trout are found in the stream only below this waterfall, although there is plenty of good water above. They appear to be something more than rainbow trout, many of them having the bright golden-yellow bellies of the Gila hybrids. Others have the bright green backs of rainbows. They are fine fish, active in the shady canyon all summer long; I have caught them as large as 15 inches.

An avid fly-fishing friend, now relocated to southern Colorado, used to avoid most small streams and side canyons in the Gila country. His complaint was that there is nowhere for the fish to swim once it is hooked. I can see his point. In some of the overlooked waters of the Mogollons I have seen large fish on the end of my line virtually swim out of the stream and beach themselves. Never was confinement more extreme than it was a few years ago, when I hooked a 15-inch fish in a pool between two falls on Cow Creek. This beautiful, moss-rimmed little pool had the profile of a chipped vase, filled to the brim. It was of pink rhyolite, about 6 to 7 feet deep, and you could straddle it if you weren't afraid of slipping and getting soaked and perhaps banging your knee (I did all three in time).

Catching such a big trout out of that little pool took a great deal of patience and about twenty minutes of unrelenting effort. First, it wasn't easy to hook the fish—not because it was shy, but rather because a dozen small ones kept striking the fly first. My solution was to catch the smaller fish, one by one, and deposit them into the pool above the falls, where they hid. Eventually, after its way to the nymph had been cleared, the large trout struck. Feeling the hook, it bored down to the bottom momentarily. Feeling pressure from the rod, it resurfaced, then jumped repeatedly into the air, maybe half-a-dozen to a dozen times, there being no place for it to swim. This was skillful jumping, too, for the fish could easily have landed out of the pool. It only needed a little hoop for a perfect, miniature imitation of a dolphin at Sea World.

In a wet year, the 3 to 4 miles below this waterfall will have thousands of trout. Then the stream abruptly ends, leaping clear into the bed of Sapillo Creek, in an ice-cold cylindrical jet of water about as big around as a tomato can. Years ago, while staring up at the waterspout, I noticed a slight pulse in the jet, as though it were being driven from the heart of the mountain. I tried to climb around and over it from the stream bottom, then got a case of the cautions and failed. Because of its impassible mouth, Cow Creek was, in the 1970s, briefly considered as a reintroduction site for the native Gila trout, but the authorities didn't want to remove the healthy population of wild trout in this stream.

Sheep Corral Creek

Instead, they chose a barren stretch of the Sheep Corral Creek. This is a very small stream, less than half the size of Cow Creek, of about .8 cfs of flow during dry weather. It could flow through a child's shoebox. Forming on the Pinos Altos ridge and dropping into Sapillo Creek just above the Gila River confluence, it descends from 6,700 to 5,200 feet. Closed to fishing, it holds rainbow hybrids and browns for a half-mile or so below an 8-foot waterfall. Within a one-mile reach of water above that barrier, you can find a few Gila trout to 14 inches, all descendants of Main Diamond Creek stock. This reach has a few natural pools and plenty of log structures designed to scour new ones. The riparian bottom of the narrow canyon contains Arizona alder, Gambel oak (an indicator of high rainfall and cool temperatures in the Gila), plus Arizona walnut, sycamore, and box elder. Of these, only the alder is strictly a streamside plant.

Cattle were a real problem here in the 1970s, but the Cow Creek grazing permit has changed hands, a vicissitude allowing for current improvement in stream conditions and continued survival of the Gila trout living here. I count no less than twelve natural trout streams in the Pinos Altos Range, in varying condition and of varying quality. Of these, Sheep Corral is one of the very smallest and poorest—small and unimportant enough for the Gila trout.

Meadow Creek

Yet another stream arising in the Pinos Altos Range north of Silver City is Meadow Creek. It is a larger, less wild, and more abused version of the little canyons entering the lower box canyon of the Gila River. After arising near the base of 9,000-foot Signal Peak and gathering intermittent tributaries, the stream struggles along in a semi-open, hideously overgrazed "meadow" (i.e., weedy clearing). From here it passes the remains of an old scout camp, then falls into a narrow little box and continues its way down for about 7 miles into Sapillo Creek.

It is rough and uninviting to follow the stream past the scout camp, partly because the fish are farther down (although eventually you find a few). The entire length of the box is narrow and steep (impassable to cattle from above), north-sloping and north-flowing, so there is a bit of living space for streamside greenery. You can also drop in along Jaybird Canyon and hit the stream right where the fishing water begins. There are no trails in this part of the Pinos Altos Range.

Trout do live near the mouth of the creek. The last half-mile is on private land, which limits access; but if you're a masochist, it's possible for you to bushwhack your way around the property line. In the scattered deep pools of the lower canyon are wild brown trout, little-known

and seldom molested. Most are small; yet, typical of lower-elevation
streams in the Gila, there is always the possibility of something a bit
larger in some of the better holes—15 inches or more.

If you want to try your luck in Meadow Creek, plan to do more
walking than fishing. When there is sufficient water in the stream, as
there is during wetter-than-usual years, it is certainly worth a try. I've
fished here a few times in low water, creeping on all fours, lying prone,
face in the gravel, beside an exposed puddle, then dapping a caddis
nymph through an opening between snag, rock, and branch, occasionally pulling out a 6- or 7-inch survivor (for the small ones seem
to survive best). If you miss your opportunity, you get to walk another
100 yards to find another promising wet spot, then start crawling again.
One thing's for sure—you won't have to share any of these pools.

Hidden Streams

Other small streams drain into the lower Gila River within the Gila
Wilderness. All flow northward into the Gila River from the main east-
west ridge of the well-watered Pinos Altos Range. I'm not going to
mention these three or four by name, by way of allowing room for a
bit of adventure. A 7.5-minute USGS topo map (Granny Mountain and
Diablo Range) should give a good idea as to which canyons falling
into the river might hold fish. These provide cold permanent flow,
abundant food, good trout habitat, and populations of wild fish
upstream to the first barrier waterfalls, which can be anywhere from
200 yards to 5 miles away from the river.

These small streams are almost completely unfished and unvisited.
All are dry at the mouth, where the floods of the Gila River pile rubble and sand on the lower end before undercutting them at the river's
edge. For this reason, and because of the countless other completely
dry canyons emptying into the Gila Box, no one bothers to hike the
100 to 300 yards of dry lower bed in these streams that keep them
disguised. Once you find water, however, the change in the canyons

is complete. Each springs to life, a mini-oasis filled with buzzing insects, blooming water plants, dense, shady broadleaf groves, kingfishers and scurrying trout. It is only a 4- to 6-mile distance from the 7,500-foot ridgeline of the Pinos Altos to the river, which flows at roughly 5,000 feet in this part of the wilderness. As a result, these gemlike little streams are highly vertical, deep in shade, with narrow, twisting canyons— very fun to fish, scrambling upward from pool to hidden pool.

One of the ironies of hiking the box canyon of the Gila River is yet another "fenceline" contrast, this one between the recovering but still bare-boned river bottom, and the Eden-like plant communities you find along the side canyons. The narrow boulder-strewn canyons prohibit the river's trespassing cattle, and as a result lush plant life fills the bottom—canyon grape climbs along the mossy walls, sycamores and box elders wedge among small clefts in the rock above the water's edge, coneflowers, penstemon, and gilia fill the banks, monkeyflowers and columbines cling to shallow riffles and mark wet sinks, and beds of watercress mark spring entrances.

The size and number of fish vary with the flow of water available, but the streams are all yours to inspect—nobody, but nobody, goes up these canyons. I happened onto all of them except one by accident, and I believe I was actually the first to fish one, perhaps two of them—at least the first to take a fly rod in there. There are no trails along any of them.

All the canyons entering the lower part of the Gila River from the north (i.e., from the Diablo Mountains and Granny Mountain) seem to have at least some water and falls too, although, like the streams entering on the other side, most are dry for their lower quarter-mile or more. Although I have found no trout in these canyons, they are a topographic mirror image of those draining the other side of the river. They drain south-facing slopes containing Emory oak, sotol, manzanita, and juniper, as opposed to the dense forests of ponderosa pine and even Douglas fir that creep down from the ridgetops into the canyons on the north slope of the Pinos Altos. They have sycamores and other deciduous canopy, as well, but apparently only a very few dace live here. The only stream on the north side that does hold fish is Turkey Creek (treated elsewhere), a major drainage that cuts into intervening mountains. Still, these canyons have not been completely inspected, at least not by me.

CHAPTER SIX

Streams of the Black Range

Rio Mimbres

Location: Aldo Leopold Wilderness, Gila National Forest, Grant County

Maps: Aldo Leopold Wilderness and Gila NF Visitors Map; Truth or Consequences and Hatch titles, USGS 1:100,000 series

Elevation: 6,200–9,000 feet

Length: 20 miles

Best times: May–October

Fish Species: Chihuahua chub, Rio Grande sucker, rainbow trout, rainbow-Gila-? trout

Fishable Tributaries: North Fork, South Fork, McKnight Canyon, N. McKnight, S. McKnight, Allie Canyon, Bear Canyon, Monument Canyon

The Black Range is dry on its eastern, Rio Grande slope. As mentioned earlier, Lt. William H. Emory of the Kearny Expedition crossed several clear streams as he followed the prairie benches at the eastern base of the range for 50 to 60 miles—and this was in October of 1846, following at least a month of drought. All are dry arroyos today, even in the rainy season.

Many streams flowing into the Rio Grande in the northern Black Range may at one time have contained trout populations, probably Rio Grande cutthroats. At the present time, however, none are known to contain anything more than small minnow and sucker species. In the southern portion of the range, two well-hidden stream systems, those of Las Animas and Tierra Blanca Creeks, discussed below, do hold trout.

The Rio Mimbres (River of Willows) does not flow into the Rio Grande, but rather into a desert basin in Mexico. It arises in the Black Range just across the Continental Divide from Las Animas Creek, first flowing north, then west, then south, acquiring such tributaries as Middle and North Mimbres and McKnight Canyon (also called the East Fork of the Mimbres). Its water often dies out in the sand and gravel somewhere between Sherman, New Mexico, and the City of Rocks State Park. Farther south, at the base of the Florida Mountains, even the channel fades away, only to reappear as mudholes in the main street of Palomas, the border town of Chihuahua.

In 1846, Lieutenant Emory wrote that he had seen trout in the Rio Mimbres, probably a bit below San Lorenzo:

Its valley was truly beautiful, about one mile wide, of rich, fertile soil, densely covered with cottonwood, walnut, ash, etc. It is a rapid, dashing stream, about fifteen feet wide and three deep, affording sufficient water to irrigate its beautiful Valley. It is filled with trout.

If one accepts that the lieutenant actually saw trout in the Mimbres (I'm suggesting that he did), it would be interesting to speculate as to what species they were. First, there is no unanimous agreement as to whether the Rio Mimbres lies east or west of the Continental Divide. It flows, or once did flow, into a closed desert basin in northern Chihuahua, Mexico, whose low point is the Laguna de Guzman, a permanent bolson lake, 5 miles long, 2.5 miles wide, and 1 to 3 feet deep. If this basin were to be filled with water, most (but not all) observers believe it would first spill over into the Rio Grande watershed. Furthermore, the headwaters of the Rio Casas Grandes, a Mexican stream also emptying into the Laguna de Guzman, contain an endemic trout distinct from but related to the Gila trout. Perhaps the Rio Mimbres seen by Emory also contained this fish, making it the fifth species of

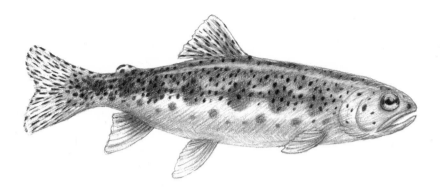

Yaqui Trout

trout native to New Mexico. Not yet scientifically described, this fish is today known as the Yaqui trout.

Lower Mimbres runs through private land with very limited public access. Permission is required. Upper Mimbres, in the Gila forest, is accessible from the Mimbres Ranger Station. Take NM 35 4 miles north. Then turn north on Forest Road 150 (the road to Wall Lake). Seven miles from here Forest Road 150A leads to Cooney undeveloped campground, right on the river. To go farther upstream into the Aldo Leopold Wilderness you need to go a mile past the Cooney turnoff and find the Forest Trail 77 trailhead. This meets the river a mile above Cooney Campground and follows it all the way to its source.

The uppermost 9 miles of the Rio Mimbres headwaters (all in a narrow canyon lined with willows and set in spruce-fir, mixed conifer, and open ponderosa timber) lie within the Aldo Leopold Wilderness. This upper reach above the mouth of Cooney Canyon holds many small wild trout, some of which, in the highest headwaters, contain pale orange cutthroat markings. A forest fire in 1994 killed fish in the Mimbres above the North Fork, traditionally the best fishing stretch, but the stream should recolonize itself naturally within a couple of years. The hybrids in the North Fork remain.

Below Cooney Canyon, the Mimbres enters heavily grazed ponderosa and juniper grasslands at 6,700 feet and loses most of its fish. Soon the water sinks from sight, flowing under gravel alluvial deposits for several miles, until it emerges above bedrock just upstream from the Gila National Forest boundary. Below this point, the valley opens up. Much unseen water enters the basin, and the river, now a good-sized stream, flows through a few well-tended *ranchitos* and is entirely on private land. Trailer parks and subdivisions start to crop up on a small plain on the river's west side, north of San Lorenzo; then the river is almost entirely forgotten.

McKnight Canyon

McKnight Canyon parallels, and is a miniature version of, the Mimbres. It drains off the southern end of McKnight Mountain, the Mimbres draining the northern and western slope. McKnight joins Mimbres just above the Gila National Forest boundary, but is intermittent for its lower 6 miles. It flows through true cattle country—the Powderhorn, East Canyon, and Mimbres Grazing Allotments.

In 1970, four years after the Gila trout had been placed on the U.S. Fish and Wildlife Service's Red List of rare and endangered species, McKnight was chosen as a transplant site for fish from Main Diamond Creek—the first relocation of Gila trout since the turn of the century. Since then the Gila National Forest has maintained a policy of "non-use" for the pastures within the Powderhorn Allotment that contained McKnight Canyon, although cattle still regularly trespass into the Powderhorn Canyon Allotment from adjacent grazing areas. Willows have been planted, and current deflectors and check dams have been installed. The stream quality within the canyon has improved greatly under this regime, and McKnight remains to date the most significant recovered habitat for the Gila trout, in spite of repeated floods (including one in 1988 that blew out improvement structures and killed many fish). Some Gilas occasionally stray below the barrier falls, located several miles above McKnight's mouth, and into the Mimbres, making their way downstream for perhaps a mile or so. The entire stream is closed to fishing.

McKnight Canyon has two tributaries also holding Gila trout—North Fork and South Fork McKnight Canyon. The South Fork holds 2 miles of trout habitat, the North Fork about a half-mile, and small numbers of Gila trout now live throughout these two reaches. The fish in the canyon and its branches run small; a few larger specimens reach up to 13 inches. The fish I have seen in the stream run from 5 to 9 inches, much like those in Main Diamond Creek, where the plantings originated.

Las Animas Creek

The Black Range is especially dry on its eastern face, where it trails off to low-lying desert foothills; on this side are only a handful of permanent stream systems, hidden way up high. To my knowledge, only two of these, Tierra Blanca Creek and the Animas system, support anything like a trout fishery.

Las Animas Creek, much the larger of the two but still quite small, is a remarkable place, a sort of living museum. Tucked into a steep, sheltered canyon formed by an indentation in the Continental Divide, it flows for nearly 10 miles north to south, and from nearly 9,000 to 6,000 feet through the interior of the Black Range. From here it turns eastward, cutting a canyon beneath semi-arid creosote foothills leading on into Caballo Reservoir. It now flows year-round only in its upper reaches. In summertime it is often precariously low, even in the high mountains. In some headwater sections, discrete pools sit as depressions interrupting a dry, bleached gravel streambed.

There is more to this state of affairs than meets the eye, however. The spots of water, connected by subsurface flow, remain cool, clean, and freshly oxygenated. Also, remarkably, these same pools hold fish—trout, in fact, seemingly well-adapted to conditions that would be the undoing of most fish species. No matter how bad the drought, the trout of Las Animas seem to reproduce with unfailing success every year.

What is just as remarkable, although certainly logical, is the fact that these seemingly vulnerable fish could be among the last of the pure-strain endemic trout of the Gila Forest, having become so suited to the

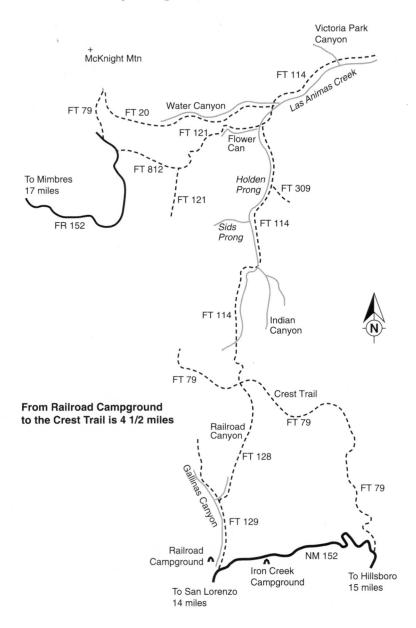

Holden Prong and Las Animas Creek

difficult conditions here that no other salmonid forms have been able to get a toehold. Most remarkable of all is the fact that these are cutthroats, far away from where cutthroats are supposed to be.

It is still an unsettled question as to whether that particular population originally existed in the stream or was put there during the fish-planting mania at the turn of the century. If the Animas fish are true natives (as many believe), then they have survived about 100 miles removed from the closest accepted natural occurrence of Rio Grande cutthroat trout in Bonito Creek, near Ruidoso. They would also be the most southerly known natural occurrence of cutthroat trout, the true native trout of the Rocky Mountains—quite appropriate, because the Black Range is the southernmost major mountain range in the Rockies. There is historical mention of trout even farther south, in the Limpia River in the Davis Mountains of Texas and also in the Devils River system in the limestone-capped Edwards Plateau, both of which populations would in all likelihood have been Rio Grande cutthroats as well.

Even after many years of stocking exotic species—browns, rainbows, and even Gila trout—the population retains all the characteristics of pure-strain Rio Grande cutthroats. Only the Gila plants seem to have taken to any degree; a few trout with Gila characteristics share the waters with the cutthroats in one tiny headwater tributary. The threat of exotic plantings continues today. The lower end of the stream on the boundary of the Gila National Forest is reportedly being stocked with exotic trout on private land.

In spite of its apparent vulnerability, Las Animas remains one of the best streams in the area. Because of its location within the Aldo Leopold Wilderness, the steep terrain above it, and the 2,000-foot average depth of its middle canyon, Las Animas receives limited use, keeping the supply of catchable fish in line with demand. This could of course change markedly within the next decade or two.

If conditions are right on the Animas (read "wet year," particularly with good summer monsoon rains), you can find fish in the 13-inch range and down, with an occasional lunker of 15 or even 16 inches. If

West Fork of the Gila River near Jenks Cabin

you pack into the Animas first during May and then September of the same year, you can actually see the summer's growth reflected in the increased average size, 6 to 7 inches versus 8 to 10. In dry years, the Animas trout populations plummet and the stream should not be fished.

Wet years are a different story. You can easily march upstream catching and releasing ten to fifteen fish in less than half an hour. You will find larger, overlooked fish in such side canyons as South Animas and Sid's Prong in the upper headwaters, and the prime fishing continues all the way down and into Victoria Park Canyon, not far from the Animas' departure from the mountains. What is even better, the cutthroats will take both wet and dry patterns most of the day. The first two or three fish from each willow-bordered run or pool will scare the rest away.

The Animas system lies within the Aldo Leopold Wilderness, and all access is by trails. The most common way to reach the main Holden Prong branch is via the Water Canyon Trail (FT 20) from McKnight Road (FR 152). McKnight Road is reachable 2 miles north from the Mimbres Ranger Station on NM 35. The turnoff is not well marked. Turn east, crossing the Mimbres River, and continue some 20 miles to the end of the road. From here follow the Crest Trail (FT 79) for 1.5 miles to the Water Canyon Trail junction. The creek is 5 miles from the junction, a rugged 3,500-foot descent.

Another way to get to the Animas is via its headwaters. To do this you can start either at Emory Pass or Railroad Campground, both on NM 152 in the Black Range. It's a 13-mile hike from Emory Pass over Forest Trail 79 (using a shortcut on trail 412, around Hillsboro Peak) and down Forest Trail 114. The other option is a 7-to-8-mile hike from Railroad Campground on Forest Trails 129, 128, and 412 to get to the first water. The first fish are below a falls at the head of Holden Prong.

The experience of both wilderness and wilderness fishing cannot be diluted. You can't properly share a narrow, solitary canyon, and when you can see a 13-inch native cutthroat trout in the water and catch it at will, you know that few people have been where you stand. Removing the fish from the stream or even hooking it—which is as easily done as thought about—doesn't seem nearly as important as having found it there, living its own life. Too few things in this world are as they should be, or where they belong.

Tierra Blanca Creek

Tierra Blanca Creek drains eastward from Sawyers Peak to the Rio Grande in the southern end of the Black Range. It flows down from 7,400 to 6,000 feet through a narrow, tree-lined, limestone-bottomed canyon not readily accessible to cattle. It is accessible either from the lower end via Forest Road 522 west of Kingston, or from the upper end via Forest Road 886 above the Royal John Mine site south of San Lorenzo, which is essentially a jeep trail in its upper end.

In 1987 and 1988 I heard scattered second- and third-hand reports of a little trout stream in the southern end of the Black Range. My hope was that it contained a relict population of Rio Grande cutthroats. Finding one other stream in the Black Range with native cutthroats would at least add another large piece to the historical puzzle. No one I spoke to knew exactly where the stream was; a few thought it was just one of several hidden side canyons of Las Animas Creek. Eventually I became convinced that it was Middle Tierra Blanca Creek, which, when compared to all other drainages south of Emory Pass, seemed to have the best chance of holding fish. And so up and over the main ridge of the Black Range I went with a friend in 1993, carrying light fly rod and day pack. It was a blistering August afternoon, after the summer rains had ceased.

As we made our way past the end of the jeep track and down into the head of the narrow canyon a mile or two below, I looked down into the first large pool and saw several trout cruising restlessly. Climbing down a rock face, I frantically tossed a fly—the first I could find and figure-eight onto my tippet—straight down into the pool. Instantly I lofted a healthy, glimmering trout out of the water. I held my breath— was it a Rio Grande cutthroat? No such luck, it was a rainbow.

My companion and I fished down, fooling unwary rainbows up to 13 inches with far too much ease. Soon we just watched the fish as we walked along. They showed great variety in color and markings, including several with the tell-tale yellow bellies, showing possible Gila trout influence. We followed the canyon all the way down to its lower end, where a few stranded fish struggled in equally stranded pools of water; and then the valley opened, the stream dried completely, and we saw our first cows lolling under the shade—all signs portending no more trout stream.

During wet years the trout seem to extend a bit farther downstream, to within striking distance of the stream crossing of Forest Road 522, which accesses the eastern flank of the Black Range south of NM 90. You can reach this road via the Hillsboro-Nutt road (NM 27).

Are there any other streams out there with Rio Grandes? I'm not sure. Cuchillo Negro, North Palomas, Circle Seven, Chloride, and Turkey Creeks, Morgan Run, and others have at least some potential as trout habitat. The Hermosa Allotment, in the midst of ten years of grazing rest, could provide recovery for North Seco Creek. At the very least, it's pretty clear that Tierra Blanca Creek would make a suitable Rio Grande cutthroat reintroduction site.

CHAPTER SEVEN

Mogollon Creek System

Mogollon Creek

Location: Gila Wilderness, Gila National Forest, Grant and Catron Counties

Maps: Gila NF Visitors Map; Mogollon Mountains title, USGS 1:100,000 series

Elevation: 5,800–7,500 feet

Length: 15 miles (fishable length)

Best Times: May–October

Fish Species: brown trout, rainbow trout, Gila trout hybrids, Gila trout

Fishable Tributaries: Rain Creek (plus one subtributary), West Fork Mogollon Creek (plus one tributary), and Lookout Canyon are open to fishing. South Fork Mogollon Creek, Trail, Corral, Woodrow, Gobbler and Turnbo Canyons, plus one headwater tributary, are all closed to protect Gila trout populations

Other Streams: Sacaton Creek (closed—Gila trout), plus Turkey Creek and the following tributaries: Sycamore (plus one unnamed branch), Manzanita and Miller Springs Canyons, plus two unnamed branches.

Trout-filled Mogollon Creek flows below the southeast flank of 10,770-foot Mogollon Baldy and heads in the ponderosa-topped crags of the Diablo Mountains, a lower-elevation companion range to the Mogollons. As it leaves the shadow of these two ranges, it turns abruptly to the

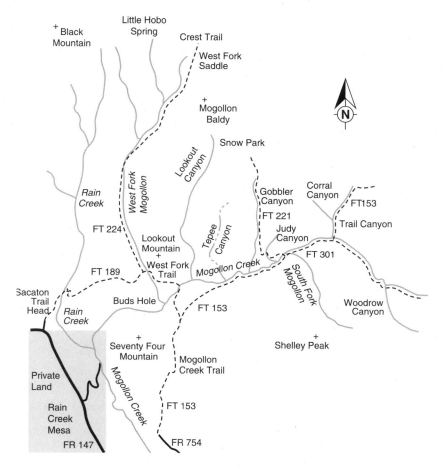

Mogollon, West Fork Mogollon, and Rain Creeks

southeast and becomes intermittent after a few miles. From here the stream follows its own peculiar hidden valley carved beneath the mesquite-filled natural prairies of Rain Creek Mesa, finally emptying into the Gila where the big river leaves its own canyon carved under the Pinos Altos Range.

This stream is neither a higher- nor typical lower-elevation habitat, but something in between. All the tributaries of Mogollon Creek are definitely colder than the main stream. Most of the water of Mogollon Creek lies between 5,500 and 6,800 feet, giving it an intermediate nature—a lower-elevation stream containing surprisingly high trout populations—much like its twin and counterpart, Turkey Creek (although Turkey Creek has a good number of warm-water species in its lower reaches). Both creeks flow southwest, carrying a current of 3 to 5 cfs or a bit more, the low-elevation divide of the Diablo Range marking a boundary between them.

The middle canyon of Mogollon Creek above Rain Creek mouth is filled with scrub oak, beargrass, false mock orange, and other dryland species on the south-facing side, while the north-facing slopes and all narrow side canyons are filled with ponderosa, Douglas fir and cool-climate Gambel oak. The Mexican black hawk, lover of desert rivers, is found in the canyon, feeding on its share of trout, whistling warnings to all fishermen who intrude. The canyon floor contains many young cottonwoods along the level flood banks wherever space allows; in the narrows only willows and occasional alders seem able to take hold. High flows can scour the narrow canyon, stripping and piling the willows. Cattle are also allowed in Mogollon Creek below Judy Canyon mouth; use is occasional, limited to choice flats.

All told, the lower 10 miles of Mogollon lose water in the summer months, although the upper stream holds from 15 to 16 miles of fishable water and receives the flow of a total of at least ten tributaries and subtributaries also capable of supporting trout. Barrier falls keep fish out of the upper reaches of most small feeder streams. Those streams entering from the north plunge off the southern face of the Mogollons, making it exceedingly difficult to follow upstream without getting "boxed." Some fall directly into the bed of the main stream. The easiest to follow are the two major lower tributaries, Rain Creek and West Fork Mogollon Creek, which have the greatest cutting power. Only these two have cut far enough into the mountain to allow hiking along lengthy portions of their streambeds. Even Mogollon Creek itself has short sections that require wading, swimming, or rock climbing to get around. The northern tributaries all have sections that need to be climbed into and out of from neighboring ridge tops.

Gila trout were reported to have been planted in the Mogollon Creek system in 1915. The watershed was stocked annually with Gila and some rainbow trout from horseback by the state until 1946 or so, after which time only rainbows were planted in the same waters. Today's fish show the whole spectrum of coloration and spotting patterns from Gila trout to hybrid to rainbow, with the more inaccessible waters and higher tributaries often resembling the native species to a greater degree. The main and south branches of Mogollon Creek also hold brown trout, which have taken hold sometime since the 1940s. The uppermost, eastern reaches of the watershed hold protected populations of pure-strain Gilas.

The main Mogollon Creek has quite a different fishing character from that of its large tributaries. The canyon it follows is much broader, the stream larger and not falling nearly as far—a relatively modest 2,000 feet in the 12 miles above its bend, as compared to the spectacular 5,000-foot drop of the West Fork and comparable decline of Rain Creek.

The presence of browns has an even more telling effect on the stream. These wary fish are safe from the casual fisherman. In the lower and middle reaches of the stream are browns up to 20 inches, even in the heavily fished section below a picture-book, 20-foot waterfall just inside the Gila Wilderness boundary. These browns share the water with the hybrids, many of which they eat. As a result, you will generally only see five or so fish in an average good-looking pool, as compared to the one to two dozen you can often find in neighboring Turkey Creek, which has no browns. You will also have to work a good part of the afternoon for a dozen fish on Mogollon, whereas you could easily catch and release three times that many on upper Turkey Creek.

Mogollon Creek has enough flow and food to allow both species to exist simultaneously in the same water, a situation not often occurring other than in the Gila River and its forks—different species generally don't share the same water in the smaller streams there. Some of the hybrids in Mogollon Creek have an interesting "mask" formed by black spots on each side of the pupil of the eye, something reported only on the Apache trout thus far. One of the upper falls, a 20-footer, is the planned protective barrier for a new upstream reintroduction of Gila trout.

One of the best ways to investigate the Mogollon Creek system is to hike over the Diablos, starting from the Sacaton Road (FR 147) north of Cliff, turning off on Forest Road 754 (marked by a sign as the "916 Ranch" road), which ends as a trailhead on lower Mogollon Creek. The trail, FT 153, climbs through cow pastures over a low ridge just below 74 Mountain, then descends into the canyon of upper Mogollon Creek, finally following the stream for several miles before ascending Turnbo Canyon and climbing over into the Gila River's West Fork drainage. Once you climb out of the canyon of Mogollon Creek and cross over to the the forested, un-park-like McKenna Park, another trail follows the West Fork Gila downstream for 15 miles before exiting the wilderness at the Gila Cliff Dwellings. By using this route, you can get to know two of the best trout streams in the Gila, Mogollon Creek and the West Fork. Thanks to seventy years of wilderness designation and closure of much of Mogollon Creek and all of the West Fork to grazing, the fishing in these streams is nearly as good as ever.

In the upper waters of Mogollon Creek, native Gila trout predominated for several years in the closed water above spring-fed Trail Canyon. Here, just upstream from the entrance of that small tributary, is a low falls acting as a natural barrier. The area above the falls was reclaimed for Gilas in the late 1980s, though browns later invaded. Trail Canyon itself, which drops into the Mogollon Creek over a 6-foot falls, has been reclaimed also, although most of the fish here are confined to the last 100 yards of the canyon below large, in-bed springs. A few Gilas can be spotted up as far as Corral Canyon, and in Corral Canyon itself, if you really want to stretch your definition of a trout stream beyond reasonable bounds.

Farther upstream are a few more trout hidden away in another micro-tributary, 3-mile-long Woodrow Canyon. In 1988, when the Gila Trout Recovery Team first reclaimed Mogollon Creek, they overlooked this stream, which shows how well hidden wild trout can be in the Diablos and Mogollons. Farther up yet, above Turnbo Canyon, Mogollon Creek becomes intermittent, with some additional, marginal trout water farther up at the forks near the head of the stream. Fish populations are low here.

Following a major fire in 1996, efforts have been made to reclaim the entirety of Mogollon watershed above Teepee Canyon, which is welcome news. Although nice browns formerly lived in this portion of the stream, and in the tributary South Fork of the Mogollon, there are countless places where this exotic can be found today, but only a handful where Gila trout belong. In addition, area streams containing Gilas provide potential for far more fishing than any brown trout water— first, because the Gilas are better able to utilize the water and, second, because they are easier to catch.

Although the entire upper Mogollon system is currently closed to fishing, I cannot help but think that at some time the stream will be reopened. At that point you will be able to try your hand at catching wild Gilas from 10 to 14 inches all along the upper Mogollon, and perhaps even in the West Fork of the Gila. A few decades ago, natives of up to 16 inches were found in both streams, some even larger in the West Fork.

West Fork of Mogollon Creek and Rain Creek

Both Rain and West Mogollon Creeks are beautiful streams, running swiftly and falling over slabs of green basalt, red rhyolite, and pink and sienna volcanic conglomerate, the bottom swept nearly clean. Both have carved spectacular canyons. I never cease to be amazed at how such a minuscule stream as Rain Creek can carve such a dizzying rent in the side of a mountain as it has onto the precipitous south slope of Mogollon Baldy. Technically, the canyon it has carved is called the Mogollon Canyon, while the canyon carved by Mogollon Creek itself is left without a name.

In their upper reaches, these streams don't so much flow as fall. Fishing in them is like climbing miles and miles of watery stairs. Unlike their counterparts in the northern Rockies, the plunging headwaters in these sun-blessed Mogollon Mountains are not to be ignored. Wherever trout can swim or swim to, you'll find them able to feed and grow. The first accounts of fishing in the West Fork report that the trout were many and small, and that is still the case today in much of the lower stream, which empties into Mogollon Creek in a deep cavern called Bud's Hole. About 6 miles above this spot the stream passes through a canyon so deep and narrow that the water remains in nearly perpetual shade, even on bright summer afternoons. As a curious result of the darkness, fish in this stretch of water are themselves very dark colored—an interesting case of "melanism" and natural selection—in contrast to the small pale fish which live over the tile-green bottoms of many of the pools lower down.

On the whole, you can expect to catch rainbows and hybrids in the Mogollon Creek system. It is no great trick to catch and release some twenty 6- to 7-inchers in an hour's time on the West Fork of Mogollon Creek, which has 11 miles of plunging, trout water, plus a nearly inaccessible, staircase tributary entering from the west (also holding trout below its lowest falls).

In the upper section of the West Fork, the trail lies 400 or more feet above the stream. If you want to make the climb down and back up, you can find some half-dozen major pools in the so-called potholes section of the canyon. The potholes are each the size of a small swimming pool and up to 15 feet deep. If you're determined to fish them all, you'll have a tough climb around many falls, and then eventually you have to climb back up to the canyon rim.

Most people get to this part of the wilderness on horseback, camping nearby and spending a day working the water below. Fishermen find a convenient ledge above the canyon from which their horses are reluctant to stray. In this section, too, the fish start to look much like their black-spotted native ancestors, occasionally ranging up to 13 inches, a size large enough for you to see yellow cutthroat markings, deep golden-yellow and olivaceous coloring, and purple iridescent sheen. In Rain Creek, with its 7 to 8 miles of water, a pattern common to many Gila headwater streams holds—the farther up you go, the more the trout begin to resemble the native Gilas. Fish in these upper reaches seem to average a bit larger than those in the West Fork, possibly because there is no developed trail and the going is considerably slower. Once you ascend the creek, you return the way you came. I've found trout of 12 inches in the higher reaches of the stream, but an acquaintance reports a 16-inch fish caught higher up yet. The west trout-bearing branch is way up the stream. It holds larger ones also. The fish are invariably small in the vicinity of the Forest Trail 169 crossing above Sacaton Road (FR 147).

Turkey Creek

Turkey Creek is a high-quality, ungrazed stream (since the 1960s at least), arising in the heart of the Diablo Range just below White Pinnacle. The stream gets its first water at about 7,400 feet, then turns to flow southwesterly through its own pink-hued, mountain-walled canyon. Finally it passes through a pristine, low-elevation, riparian *bosque* at 4,700 feet before joining the Gila River, just 7 or 8 miles above the lower end of the Gila's own box canyon. The slopes above most of the stream consist of piñon, juniper, scrub oak, manzanita, sotol, and prickly pear. The upper zones hold ponderosa pine. About 20,000 acres of the upper watershed burned in a 1993 fire, which does not appear to have affected the streams below.

Forest Trail 155, once a main route into the Gila Wilderness but now seldom traveled, follows the length of Turkey Creek, although climbing above it for a few miles above Skeleton Canyon. A side trail (FT 158) branches off to ascend Sycamore Canyon. All other tributaries of Turkey Creek are without trails. To find Forest Trail 155, take the Turkey Creek Road (NM 153, alias FR 155) north of the town of Gila, and follow it north to its bitter end at the Gila River, roughly 25 miles from Gila village. It is steep and can be washed out after heavy rains (check with locals after snowmelt or during the summer rains). You then ascend the Gila River for 1.5 miles, wading across the river three times, to the usually dry mouth of Turkey Creek. Here Forest Trail 155 begins. The Sycamore Creek trail (FT 158) is 6 miles from here, the head of Turkey Creek about 20 miles. Hiking into upper Turkey gives you an immediate appreciation as to how lonely and rugged the Gila country can be.

Turkey Creek is a sort of twin to Mogollon Creek in the southern boundary of the Mogollon Mountains, just as Whitewater Canyon is twin to Mineral Creek in the northern end. It contains smallmouth bass, warm-water, nongame species, and rainbows below Skeleton Canyon in its lower end. You can find roundtail chubs and rainbow-Gila hybrids in the middle reaches, and Gila hybrids in its upper reaches. All together, it has about 13 miles of trout water.

In the summer, Turkey Creek is usually dry for a quarter-mile or so above its mouth, but above this are bass (some surprisingly large), round-tail chubs, suckers, and also a few trout, right up to the mouth of the fishless, but usually flowing, Skeleton Canyon. For the next 1.5 miles Turkey Creek has no fish to speak of—at least not in summer—just tadpoles, bullfrogs, and a very rare chub. This, I am sure, is due to the influence of one of the largest and hottest hot springs in the region (measured at 160 degrees), which pours into Turkey Creek at the upper end of this barren stretch. Apparently, both surface and subsurface flows from Skeleton Canyon cool and freshen Turkey Creek sufficiently well to allow abundant numbers of fish to return to the stream, mainly the warm-water species.

Generally speaking, the only humans visiting the Turkey Creek area will be seen here and downstream near the Gila River. A few years ago I startled a group of very suspicious sun worshippers while passing through to get at the excellent fishing above. Not many other fly fishermen have passed the spot since.

Conditions below the hot spring and in the lower creek give no clue as to how good the upper stream is. Above the hot springs, trout predominate. The section between Sycamore Canyon and the hot springs is excellent water and lightly fished, not being accessible by trail and lying at the bottom of an unscalable box canyon. Trout cannot easily move upstream from the river mouth past the hot water, at least not during normal streamflow, and this has helped keep rainbow hybridization lower in the upper Turkey Creek than in other streams in the Mogollons. Current hatchery plantings into the Gila River cannot, in all likelihood, move up Turkey Creek. This in turn is one good reason why the small fish in the upper reaches and tributaries of this watershed resemble actual Gila trout, while fish in the middle reaches (up to 14 inches in length) vary widely in coloration. They resemble what geneticists call a "hybrid swarm," affected by rainbows planted in the stream's middle reaches from the 1930s through the 1950s.

In addition to the mainstem, I've found five upper tributaries containing Gila-type trout, the most notable being pristine Sycamore Canyon, a pure water source falling through a narrow defile from 7,500 to 6,000 feet. The canyon is shaded over with sycamores, chokecherries, New Mexico alders of up to 40 feet, Arizona walnut trees, willows, bigtooth maples, gooseberries, elderberry shrubs, narrowleaf cottonwoods, box elders, and canyon grape arbors. It has its own mini-fork, way up under the big dividing ridge of the Diablos, for the delight of connoisseurs of truly tiny things. Both headwater branches form off the crest of the Diablo Range, joining to flow south 5 miles or so and providing some of the finest native trout habitat in the Southwest.

The trout in upper Sycamore are not fished for often and attain amazing sizes—13 and 14 inches in a good wet year by late fall. These fish often bear all the markings attributed in the literature to mature Gila trout, even the garb of spawning males. These include a dark, olivaceous color above the lateral line, a dusky golden, enamel-like belly and venter, yellow-orange cutthroat markings, creamy fin edges, and a faint, iridescent purple sheen appearing irregularly across the sides. The 12- to 14-inch fish have somewhat larger, sparser spots than those of lesser size and age.

In some stretches the water of Sycamore Canyon is so slight that fish seem to be out of place, to have been merely deposited there. In the upper end there are fish in wet pockets between dry gravel beds; lower down, where the flow picks up, their backs bulge out of the water as they race after food. As you approach them they turn sideways to wriggle under a stone, in the manner of a salamander hiding on a damp forest floor.

Similar conditions hold in Miller Springs Canyon, entering upper Turkey Creek from the south, although it falls less and flows lower (in both elevation and volume), and its trout are more rainbowlike. Smaller tributaries where trout can be found from time to time include Manzanita Canyon, where I have caught hybrids to 10 inches, and a small unnamed tributary entering from the north just downstream from Miller Springs Canyon, where Gila trout look-alikes can be found. Another fork near the head of Turkey Creek also holds these fish.

Sacaton Creek

Sacaton Creek is a small gem of a stream flowing off the south end of Sacaton Mountain. In appearance it is a miniature version of Rain Creek, with pink and lime-green sculpted rock pools, sprinkled with brightly colored, fine grained and slowly moving caddis larvae cases. These seem to collect the lightest, brightest granules off the streambed for their cladding, making them stand out clearly. Permanent flow of the stream is about 2 miles, the upper end among spectacular rock bluffs, the lower end through very deeply shaded pine and Douglas fir. Fishing water ranges from 6,600 to 8,000 feet. The stream disappears just above a natural waterfall, where almost all the water is diverted into a concrete ditch (which locals swear flows uphill) and into an open, parklike mesa, from which it more reasonably flows downhill. In 1990 upper Sacaton was stocked with forty Gila trout, which increased to a population of two to three hundred by 1993. It is currently closed to fishing.

CHAPTER EIGHT

San Francisco River System

San Francisco River

Location: Apache National Forest, Arizona; Frisco Box RARE II roadless area, Lower San Francisco RARE II roadless area, Gila National
Forest

Maps: Gila NF Visitors Map; Tularosa Mountains title, USGS
1:100,000 series

Elevation: 3,900–7,800 feet

Length: 100 miles

Best Times: May–October

Fish Species: rainbow trout, largemouth bass, smallmouth bass,
Sonoran suckers, longfin dace, roundtail chubs, loach minnow,
speckled dace, channel catfish

Fishable Tributaries: Tularosa River: Stone, Trout, Romero,
Centerfire, Cienega, Mineral, N. Mineral, S. Mineral, Apache, Negrito,
N. Negrito, and S. Negrito Creeks; Rocker, Beaverdam, Whitetail,
Whitewater, S. Whitewater, and Lipsey Canyons; Black Mountain
Prong: unnamed branch (of Whitewater)

The San Francisco drains a natural break between the Mogollons and
Arizona's Blue Range. It begins at 8,300 feet near Alpine, Arizona, and
flows through several small ranges in New Mexico's Gila National Forest
for about 100 miles, gathering abuse, flowing red with each summer
rain. After passing through the villages of Luna, Reserve, Glenwood,

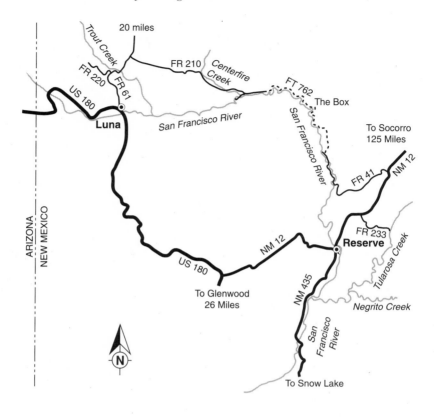

San Francisco River from Luna to Reserve

and intervening roadless mountains, the river bends west at the Frisco Hot Springs, re-enters Arizona at 3,800 feet, then descends 50 miles through one of the wildest, least-visited box canyons left in the Southwest. It is of comparable size to the Gila River where the two join below Clifton, Arizona.

Trout are not often found in this lower end, but rainbows do show up a bit farther upstream between Glenwood and Frisco Hot Springs, a section where the river is recharged with cool subsurface water. The largest share of trout are at the river's other end, 3,000 feet higher in the mountains and a good drive north of the hot springs. The uppermost reach in New Mexico descends from 7,500 to 6,500 feet. Here the San Francisco leaves an upper canyon near the Arizona state line, passing through the open Luna Valley—a high-elevation bowl surrounded by a number of small ranges—then cuts a passage leading through the San Francisco Mountains and into the very difficult Frisco Box. Throughout this descent, the river is still a true high-elevation mountain stream, with potential for superb fishing. The upper drainage is large, but precipitation is a scant 14 inches per year, which has a concentrating effect on both the stream's basic productivity and its spoil of eroded material. The water is packed with nutrients but sometimes with silt as well, and here, as below, state water-quality standards are violated.

To date, very little of the San Francisco's fishing potential has been realized. In fact, of the entire length of the river in New Mexico, the only sections traditionally of interest to trout fishermen have been the 6 miles of narrow canyon between the state line and Luna, New Mexico, and the Frisco Box section of the river a few miles below.

The trout above Luna are rainbows of up to 10 inches, with a chance of landing a 14- to 16-inch prize. No trout are stocked in the river in New Mexico, and although they are far outnumbered by suckers and disappear from long stretches during summer, the ones you do catch are generally plump and healthy.

Fishing is best in morning and evening. I fish larger nymph patterns deep and slow in the larger scoured canyon pools; some of the beaver dams in this section are also deep enough to provide fairly good, early morning fishing, in usually cloudy water. Often the fish feed heavily after heavy July and August thunderstorms, both before the river muddies and as it clears again. Even under these conditions the fish tend to avoid the shallower runs and riffles. The summer fishing in this uppermost section ends a mile or two above Luna, where water is removed for irrigation in summer. Most is returned just below the townsite on private land extending another 2 miles.

The 10-mile stretch between Luna and Frisco Hot Springs, just above the Frisco Box, has for decades been a badly degraded pasture with little fishing. To know your habitats in the Gila Forest, you first need to know the varied conditions of the corresponding grazing allotments.

This one has allowed up to 150 cows along the bank and in the water—winter, spring, summer, and fall—too much for the stream to take. The cows are less happy with the sparse grass among the pine groves than with their homestead on the green banks.

For the past 2 years, however, all cattle have been removed, triggering a resurgence of stream life. In the summer of 1995, I spotted new alder seedlings and an amazing young growth of sedges, tule rushes, cattails, and flowering buckwheat, plus several native clover and knotgrass species right at the water's edge. These plants have filtered out much of the silt in low streamside swales and small, newly created marshes. Bankside exclosures built in 1991 were filled with young willows.

The trout had also returned, in dramatic fashion, including young of the year. I landed rainbows to 16 inches in this formerly barren stream reach. Most of the trout were holed up in the deeper pools—sometimes thirty to forty of them. Populations increased steadily from Big Spring near Centerfire Creek mouth down to the Frisco Box, which has always held a moderate number of trout.

The roadless, trail-less Frisco Box, 3 miles of it, is narrow, filled with rapids and small falls, and genuinely dangerous during spring snowmelt and summer rains. Virtually all of it must be waded, under dark red pinnacles and pine-topped bluffs. Roadless Dillon Mountain looms far above, out of sight. The deep red rent the canyon makes in the San Francisco Range is visible from NM 12 near Reserve—something like the Brazos Box near Chama, New Mexico. Here willows and cottonwoods gain toeholds in cracks in rock faces and flood-borne silt deposits just slightly out of reach of the normal current. Waterfalls and logjams provide deep holes. Some sections of the box pass through walled-in eddies that reach your chest even when the river is at its lowest. During high flows the 3-mile reach is impassible and dangerous even to approach.

The stream bottom in the box is still a bit silty, but there is at least one large fish lurking in most good pools, along with several of 8 to 11 inches—and, yes, they have the faint appearance of Gila hybrid specimens. The bigger fish will take any of the various stonefly nymph patterns, as long as they are drifted near the bottom—the birdnest, copper-ribbed, or rubber-legged varieties all work. Equally effective are #8–10 Marabou Muddler or Woolly Bugger patterns with tin shot, as are smaller (sizes 14–16) beadhead caddis and mayfly nymphs. The old rule, "Bright day, dark nymph" (and vice versa), applies here. If the water is slightly cloudy, so much the better—most of the big trout I've caught on the upper San Francisco have attacked deeply fished nymphs in slightly murky water.

If you wish to explore this whole length when the river is low, it is advisable to leave a car at the lower end on Forest Road 41 out of Reserve. Get a ride to the upper end by following FR 19 some 5 miles out of Luna, then turn down FR 210 past Centerfire Bog, 8 miles or so, until the the road dead-ends right on the river. This is almost 50 miles away by auto, but only 7 or so by foot. Then, if weather permits, you hike down to your car. The box is about 3 miles downstream by trail.

At the lower end of the Frisco Box, the river flows through roughly a mile of private property. Entry along the stream is no longer allowed, but the trail continues, climbing above the northeast bank and around the property line, where it meets Forest Road 41. This will lead you back to NM 12 and to Reserve, as your Gila National Forest map will show.

After leaving the box, the San Francisco changes considerably, now passing through small lower-elevation ranges such as the Saliz and Kelley Mountains. Again, as it does upstream near Luna, the river finds an open valley between Reserve and San Francisco Plaza before cutting another 30 miles of lonely, unvisited canyon between Negrito and Pueblo Creeks. Trout are scattered in a 4-mile stretch of Forest Service land below the box, and under the Saliz Mountains below the Tularosa River—Negrito Creek confluence, with even fewer below selected rapids all the way to the US 180 bridge, 10 miles above Alma, New Mexico (population 10). Most likely, though, you would encounter none. Below the bridge, near Pueblo Creek mouth, the river valley opens up again; water is removed for irrigation, and the silt-choked stream dries up occasionally

San Francisco River above Frisco Box

in the vicinity of Alma. Even here, migrant rainbows can turn up in spring—origin unknown.

The uppermost San Francisco River is accessible via US 180 out of Luna, New Mexico. The Head of Ditch Campground provides good access just off US 180, 2 miles west of Luna. The highway also crosses the river 6 miles west of Luna. The Frisco Box section of the river is accessible from the upstream side via Forest Road 19. Take this graded gravel road 5 miles north of Luna to the Forest Road 210 turnoff, then follow FR 210 some 8 to 9 miles to its end, finding Forest Trail 762, which follows the river. The area below the Box is accessible via Forest Road 41, which enters US 180 some 5 miles north of Reserve.

Trout Creek

A notable upper tributary of the San Francisco near Luna is Trout Creek, heading on the eastern flank of 10,900-foot Escudilla Mountain. This is the same mountain on which the late Aldo Leopold learned to "think like a mountain" in the 1920s, and where he reported the last grizzly bear in Arizona to have been killed. Trout Creek holds some surprisingly large rainbow trout and many more 6- and 7-inchers. One overlooked section lies between Luna townsite and the crossing of Bill Knight Gap Road, or FR 19 (known locally as the "Road to Nowhere"). Although the creek sometimes dries up in the vicinity of the crossing, about a half-mile below the bridge are pools supporting rainbows as large as any you will find in the nearby river. Above the bridge lie several miles of fishable water, until the stream branches and subdivides in open, high-elevation cow country filled with muddy tanks.

Trout Creek is better than might be expected. During the rainy season its benches give the appearance of a tattered pool table; scattered willow clumps along the banks are hedged to the nub every spring. Like the San Francisco, upper Trout Creek is often muddy, but here, as there, are also a few beaver and a few of their ponds—enough, all told, to keep a reasonably stable population of wild fish in a stream not stocked since the mid-1970s. Few seem to show Gila-type characteristics, and in this respect they are similar to the San Francisco River specimens found near the state line. Sometimes the flow in late summer is quite low on Trout Creek, with dry reaches. At the upper end of the watershed, in places like Erin Lake, Underwood Spring, and Flannigan Cienega, grazing pressure is severe and banks are bare, yet the system flows in the 7,000–8,000-foot range and cools off every night.

Tularosa River

The Tularosa River, 25 miles long and nearly *kaput,* nonetheless yields a few trout. It feeds the San Francisco a few miles below Reserve. The minuscule "river" itself arises from a very large, 8.2 cfs spring in the bed of the Tularosa Canyon a couple of miles above Aragon. Not many rivers achieve their maximum flow at their very head, but this one does. The spring, with a temperature of 57 degrees and forming at 6,700 feet, should make for excellent trout water below. Actual conditions are a far cry from what they should be, however. The open valley of the upper Tularosa—with its trailer ranchitos, rusted car bodies, and crude billboards—provides limited open pasture while allowing sun and silt to change the essential nature of the stream. Within only a mile and a half of its source, the summer temperature of the Tularosa increases from 57 to 77 degrees.

The last several miles of the Tularosa above Reserve, New Mexico, are wild and unvisited. The stream passes through a broken-off mountain, then pours into the San Francisco River a couple of miles after receiving the cooler, cleaner flow of Negrito Creek, at an elevation of about 5,700 feet. At its mouth, the recharged river holds about 3 to 6 cfs of running water, and I've found a few nice stream-bred rainbows in this vicinity—pale, with faint yellowish traces on lower body and fins, and large, sparse spotting, complete with rosy pink redband.

Negrito Creek System

Negrito Creek, a good-sized, mid-elevation stream and major tributary of the San Francisco, drains a very large watershed—roughly 100,000 acres. It heads in the northern Mogollons off Bearwallow and Negrito Mountains, flowing north toward Reserve; it empties into the Tularosa and San Francisco Rivers a few miles below the village.

Negrito holds good flow in a roadless, trail-less lower canyon below the joining of the South Fork and the degraded North Fork (which has only a couple of miles of permanent flow, a few active beaver dams, and very limited fishing). Upstream from this point, the South Fork opens up a bit—its mini-canyon paralleled above by a graded spur (FR 503) for 6 miles or so—then meets and follows the main forest access route (FR 141) between Reserve and Snow Lake for 3 miles in an undeveloped camping and picnic area. Then South Fork branches away to the south and climbs to its headwaters off Negrito Mountain, while Forest Road 141 follows tributary Beaverdam Canyon. This upper drainage has suffered from past logging activity at the head of subtributary Ecklebarger Canyon, and still runs bright red after summer rains. Attempts are being made to replant the bottom with willows and to berm and bar the upper dry tributaries in the hope of retarding the heavy erosion. The area is part of what is called a "swing allotment," and has been partially off-limits to cattle since 1993.

A few rainbows and Gila hybrids can be found in the upper South Fork and the lower 2 miles of Beaverdam Canyon, right along FR 141. Rainbow hybrids have also been spotted in upper Rocker Canyon, a tiny headwater tributary of the South Fork descending from Corner Mountain and slated for logging. Another tributary, Gwynn Canyon, is dry but holds an unpublicized off-bed stock pond just off FR 141, occasionally stocked with rainbows, and quite popular with locals.

In the 1970s and 1980s, the section of South Negrito Creek between Beaverdam Canyon and the mouth of the North Fork was arguably the best, accessible fishing spot in the Gila Forest, but has since fallen off. Though there are still wild trout here, much of the public fishing today in the upper stream is of the put-and-take variety. In the summers of 1993 and 1994, in particular, the native Gila-rainbow hybrids were scarce, the water warm and fuzzy. Overgrazing is pronounced, changing the

plant composition on upper-elevation terraces like Rainy Mesa and seri-
ously affecting stream quality on virtually the entire upper Negrito watershed. Fenced exclosures in Sheep Basin Meadow show the incredible
vegetative growth potential still to be found in the system's long-dried,
long-altered *cienegas*.

Below the confluence of the North and South Forks, Negrito mainstem is a study in contrasts. Sonoran and desert suckers, in company
with longfin and speckled dace, outnumber trout at a ratio of perhaps
200 to 1. Yet I have seen a number of 16- to 20-inch rainbows, spooky
and extremely hard to approach, in the roadless section just below the
(utterly blown-out) Sign Camp Canyon. In places here the river banks
are stripped as bare as a sandbox. Premonsoon water temperatures can
increase to upper tolerance levels by afternoon. Oddly enough, a surprising number of the wild fish I have seen in the difficult, marginal water
of the middle and upper reaches of the main Negrito canyon show the
usual hybrid characteristics—perhaps a result of evolutionary "back-
breeding," which reinvents the originally well-adapted Gila trout.

Fortunately, several springs enter Negrito's streambed in the narrow
lower box, where you have to wade, either from below or above. It is
most productive from below, but access is a problem. I generally fish
it from the Tularosa mouth. On NM 435, south of Reserve, there's a turnoff
marked "Negrito Creek"—and that's all. You simply follow the dirt road
across the San Francisco River to its dead end, and try to make your
way upstream, avoiding all private land by following fence lines, as
others have done over the years. Access is slightly easier from above,
where you can inquire for permission at the Cullum ranch house on
the stream at the end of Forest Road 503.

The farther downstream you go from here, the better the water gets.
The Negrito Box is a typical Mogollon Mountains canyon: basalt-ribbed,
with freestone bottom, seemingly lit from below, shaded in early morning and late afternoon. The water colors soon after late summer rains
and clears slowly, meandering through ochre-colored walls at 5,200
feet, the hills above studded with piñon and juniper scrub. In spite of

all the seeming obstacles to their existence, the fish still thrive in the lower end of the stream. A few years ago I caught and released fifty or so good trout in the morning, including a number in the 14-inch class, before being drenched and sent home by an early afternoon thunderstorm. Fish are everywhere—both the dull-colored, warm-water natives massed on the bottom and the bright green rainbows drifting in the current. Even though Negrito is a few degrees warmer than is ideal, the basic fertility of this spring-fed flow is evident. Wading in the water causes a riot of fish, stirring up mud and sending waves upstream. One only wishes more of these were trout. In spite of watershed and habitat problems, it is still hard to visualize the wild trout finally disappearing from this magical, murmuring, twisting and turning lower canyon.

Whitewater Creek

Fertile Whitewater Canyon has wild trout in about 15 miles of fishable water from the Catwalk Picnic Area to its headwater reaches tucked between 10,860-foot Whitewater Baldy and 10,700-foot Black Mountain. The water stays cold all summer, from 5,100 feet at the picnic area to 9,000 feet at the trail-less, unfished upper end. This is the deepest of all the canyons—up to 3,000 feet deep—in the heart of the Mogollons, the whole stretch accessible only by foot or horseback.

A good trail (FT 207) follows the bottom from Catwalk Picnic Area all the way to the upper forks of the stream, before climbing up to 10,400-foot Hummingbird Saddle. Two side trails (FT 179 and FT 206) descend into the canyon from the Bursum Road (NM 159) on the way from Mogollon village to Snow Lake Campground.

The two trails from the Bursum Road down to Middle Whitewater are an eyeful. After climbing far down under the tremendous ridges that line the canyon on either side, only to find a relatively tiny stream below, you have a moment's discouragement, a condition soon cured, however, by the sight of trout scurrying everywhere as you approach the bank. Once you are in the canyon, it's just you and the talking stream—no room for anything else.

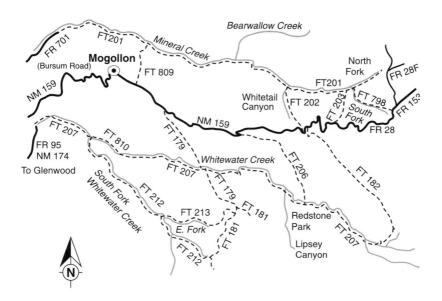

Whitewater Creek, South Fork Whitewater Creek and Mineral Creek

A more earthbound approach to the stream lies at the Catwalk—called "New Mexico's Best Kept Secret" by area Chambers of Commerce, but someone told. The recently enlarged and paved parking lot fills with cars on summer days; tourists file in and out of the canyon along the lower half-mile of the Catwalk National Recreational Trail. The trail follows Whitewater Creek along the route of an old elevated pipeline that supplied water to the now-vanished town at the mouth of the canyon.

Owing partly to the fame of the Catwalk, Whitewater is probably the most frequently fished small stream in the Gila Forest, with fishermen following its trail from end to end. In summer, the interior canyon gets fished once or twice a week, I would guess—that's crowded by Gila standards.

Deep pools in the first 1.5 miles above the picnic area at one time held some very nice fish, but today's trout seem only to get smaller every year. Farther up, crowds thin and the average size of the fish increases somewhat, but the largest ones are removed from much of this wilderness stream by steadily increasing fishing pressure.

Whitewater contains a population of Little Brown and Little Yellow Stoneflies (*Amphinemura* and *Skwala*), with hatches in early July. The trout feed vigorously if you happen to hit the water when the nymphs are emerging. Even during such times, however, the trout are not truly selective and can be caught on a number of fly patterns. I use a 6- or 7-foot rod with 2-weight line to slay the dragons here.

The canyon's sudden turn above the Catwalk, a larger version of the Devil's Elbow of the South Fork, is as beautiful a stretch of small stream as you will find anywhere. Occasionally, however, the canyon floods, washing out the road and "closing" the Catwalk, and the good old days return, briefly. On a four-day inspection of the canyon, after a 1979 closure, I caught trout up to 11 inches wherever I cast, morning, noon, and evening.

On my last visit to the Catwalk, I spotted a 7-inch hybrid trout finning in the current. My mind drifted back to the first time I camped here, alone for two days, in 1977. My first cast at this very same spot had brought a strike; it was a good fish, and I had discovered an entire mountain range. This time, however, my reverie was interrupted by the sudden appearance of a tourist asking, "Catch any?"

South Fork of Whitewater Creek

Within the Gila Wilderness, four tributaries of varying size, each containing trout, enter Whitewater Creek. The first and largest, the South Fork of Whitewater Creek, enters just a couple of miles above the Catwalk. Forest Trail 212 heads up the canyon, leading to the deeper pools in the lower 2 miles.

Small natives become very abundant just below the Devil's Elbow, a defile where the stream has cut through the Skeleton Ridge, a volcanic dike that forms the southern rim of Whitewater Canyon itself. The fish have bright orange markings on their pectoral fins, along with cream-and-orange underbellies. Their genetic composition is uncertain, although it is generally agreed that the Gila trout is represented in the mixture.

Small brook trout start to appear in the South Fork shortly upstream from the elbow and continue up through the headwaters under Nabors Mountain. The brook trout have been here many years, but, oddly enough, this species is found nowhere else in southwestern New Mexico, even though it is quite common in the Sacramento Mountains on the other side of the Rio Grande.

Brook trout predominate in the uppermost end, feeding indiscriminately on everything from stoneflies to cicadas. A few years ago I caught a 12-inch brookie in the lower end of the East Fork Whitewater Creek, an upper tributary of the South Fork at the Tennessee Meadow, as I hiked down from Camp Creek Saddle. A week later I returned and just as easily caught it again.

The trail ascending the South Fork becomes tricky as it climbs through the elbow, and horses have a habit of falling down the canyon and landing in the stream below. As you move farther up main Whitewater Canyon, 10 miles or so, you enter the compact heart of the Mogollon Mountains, country that "stands on end," as they say here. It is a country easy to see, but hard to visit. The western end of the range has very little level ground; the streams are all canyons from source to mouth, top to bottom.

Lipsey Canyon

Lipsey Canyon, which plunges down from Spruce Creek Saddle to enter the Whitewater below Redstone Park, holds a unique population of trout. It has been postulated by some observers that the trout living in this little stream are Gila-cutthroat hybrids—"Gilacuts." This unusual genetic combination is undoubtedly shared with the orange-colored fish in the main stream.

In the 1980s, the NMG&F were of the opinion that streams like Whitewater Creek were "underfished," a condition said to result in an abundance of stunted trout. Lipsey Canyon argues against such a view. Typical of many tiny tributaries, the fish here are noticeably larger than those in the main stream, running from 9 to 13 inches. The trout of

Lipsey Canyon are seldom bothered—I doubt that it gets fished for months or even years at a time—allowing them to reach full growth. Full growth for Whitewater Creek, by comparison, would probably be 17 inches or so, possibly more. In the past ten years, I have only rarely seen such fish in the upper stream.

Lipsey is hard to find. The entrance to the canyon is obscured by dense willow growth. It is equally hard to fish, tiny and heavily covered by willows and dogwood. It is so overgrown that even dapping with a 6-foot rod can be problematic.

Mineral Creek

If you want peace, quiet, and a chance to fish for small trout in New Mexico's "Next Best Kept Secret," you might want to try the Catwalk's smaller twin, Cooney Canyon, on Mineral Creek. It crosses US 180 as a dry wash just outside Alma, New Mexico, a few miles north of Glenwood.

Tucked into the northern edge of the Mogollons, Mineral is topologically and hydrologically almost identical to Whitewater Creek. The mouth of the creek is dry, otherwise there are the same 7 miles of gravel wash paralleled by a road following upstream until, at last, water appears. An abandoned mining adit, the Oaks Tunnel, provides warm-water flow just above Cooney's Tomb, named for a gold seeker of the last century. Shortly above, the road ends in a small corral and parking lot under sycamores, near the mouth of a sculpted, pink box canyon. The remains of a former mining camp, also named Cooney, lie farther upstream, similar to the old mill site 2 miles above the former town of Graham at the mouth of the Whitewater Canyon.

You can follow a crude trail upstream, passing over several small falls and native rock pools littered with pebbles, where wild trout congregate. One difference, immediately apparent, between the Catwalk and Cooney's Canyon is that the stream here, grazed in all but the narrowest portions, is far less shady. Beaver are also found upstream, or at least have been in the recent past.

The trout are similar to those in Whitewater Canyon, though a bit more like rainbows in the lower end. Higher up, however, they change, becoming yellower and more brightly spotted near the uppermost of the 13 miles of fishable water tucked between 9,950-foot Bearwallow and 9,400-foot Spring Mountains.

Like Whitewater Canyon, Mineral Creek can be followed by Forest Service trail for its entire length, with side trails (FT 202 and FT 808) descending to the canyon bottom from the Bursum Road (NM 159). Most fishermen use the lower of the two, which meets the road just above the hamlet of Mogollon. You can most easily reach the upper end of Mineral Creek by taking Forest Trail 808 from Bursum Road down Whitetail Canyon (which has a few trout in its lower end) or by dropping down from the Bearwallow Mountain turnoff (Forest Road 153) to meet the forks at the head of the stream.

Fish in this headwater area are as small as those in the Cooney Canyon stretch, but, as mentioned above, they have Gila-type characteristics. A Gila Forest biologist reported a 17-inch trout caught in the upper portion of Mineral Creek in the 1970s, above (fishless) Bearwallow Creek, but you'll be doing well to find one half that size. Typical of Mogollon fishing, you can catch them by stalking on your knees and roll casting to the middle of the larger water pockets. Less vegetation means easier casting, but poorer habitat—these streams obtain 90 percent or more of their food nutrients from deciduous plant and leaf litter falling into the stream from the banks.

Mineral Creek was chosen by the Gila Trout Recovery Team for reintroduction in 1994, but opposition by Catron County officials ended the plan. Riparian conditions on Mineral Creek are currently fair to poor, as compared to the overall good condition of Whitewater. A 1976 estimate by Paul Turner, from New Mexico State University, placed about sixteen thousand trout (including subcatchables) in the stream; he omitted in this estimate some 3 miles of stream in the vicinity of Cooney Canyon, which also holds fish. This figure represents about six times the world's population of accepted pure-strain Gila trout. Perhaps the Gilas will eventually be reintroduced into Mineral Creek, perhaps not.

Big Dry Creek

The last New Mexico trout stream to empty into the San Francisco is Big Dry Creek. The stream in the canyon is good sized, and it holds many trout—browns, basically, with a few Gila hybrids up high and Gila trout in the final 1.2-mile headwater section above a 30-foot barrier falls. This good roadless, and nearly pathless, creek is almost visible from the Aldo Leopold Vista on the National Forest boundary south of Glenwood. Seen from the Vista, a massive rock horn juts out from Sheridan Mountain, hiding the canyon bottom from view. The whole canyon of Big Dry is hidden, in fact, no matter what your vantage point— 10,750-foot Sacaton Mountain forms its south wall, 9,700-foot Holt Peak its north. In between lies the most rugged little bit of trout fishing in southern New Mexico.

Big Dry is not quite inaccessible in its middle reaches, but it isn't easy, either. There are three basic ways to approach Dry Creek, all on foot. You can follow it up from Soldiers Hill off US 180, hitting the dry bed just north of the Grant–Catron County line. Follow it upstream to the mouth of the box, where the water begins—expect a lot of wading through loose gravel. Second, you can follow a track (Forest Road 146) from the highway to the foot of the Gila Wilderness at Sheridan Corral, then take 5 miles of forest trail (Forest Trails 181, 226, and 225) along a hot juniper, prickly pear, and agave ridge, dropping into the cool walnut and box elder groves along Sheridan Canyon. Then, as you climb up over the powder-dry Sheridan Mountain with its naked groves of ponderosa pine, you despair of ever finding water, much less trout. Finally, angling into the canyon through beargrass and thickets of white oak, you can hear the stream, but you have no idea how far away or down it is. By the time you reach the old cabin at the mouth of the (fishless) North Fork, looking over the ice-cold, sparkling clear water of Big Dry, you are ready to do what some of the earlier explorers did after finding water in this water-scarce land—dive into the first pool and start gulping. In June 1985, I met a party of teenage boys who hated the prospect of climbing out of the sun-blasted canyon so much

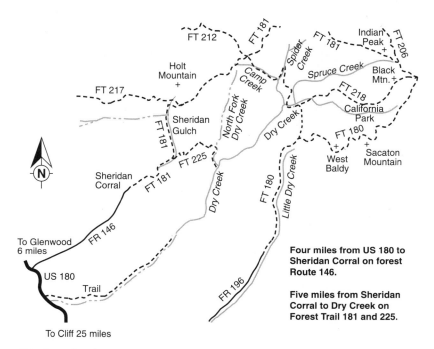

Four miles from US 180 to Sheridan Corral on forest Route 146.

Five miles from Sheridan Corral to Dry Creek on Forest Trail 181 and 225.

Big Dry Creek

that they decided to follow the stream all the way back to the highway and try to fetch a ride back to their truck.

Above North Fork mouth the canyon gets rugged quickly. There are a couple of miles of good water below, sometimes more. Like nearby Whitewater Canyon, Big Dry contains a healthy stonefly population—always a good sign to the trout fisherman. The fish in this lower section are smaller, but not at all secretive. In fact, the browns of Big Dry, while as shy as all of their kind, do feed all through the day in the shady canyon.

The third route into Big Dry gets you in touch with the biggest fish, but it's a good little climb. You follow Sacaton Road (FR 147) up the barren wash of Little Dry Creek, turn up FR 196 as it continues up the wash, then follow Forest Trail 181 as it climbs to the head, over more beargrass and oak scrub, to Windy Gap, at close to 8,400 feet. The trail continues down, down, down, into the canyon, so deep and narrow it almost seems to have been tunneled into the mountain. Here, on the north-facing canyon wall, you find shady Douglas fir groves, and mossy springs, all quite a contrast to the south-facing Sheridan Mountain Trail on the canyon's other side. When you get down to the stream at 6,700 feet, a few miles above the North Fork, you find narrowleaf cottonwood, willows, box elder, and alder trees at the trail crossing.

From the crossing you can fish without much difficulty upstream to the Golden Link Cabin, where the stream becomes steep and the posted section containing Gila trout begins. At this point, a side trail climbs away from the stream and heads to the top of the watershed at the Mogollon Crest Trail. Downstream from the trail crossing, the canyon soon becomes even steeper and makes for tricky wading and rock climbing, plus an occasional opportunity to cast. Spider Creek and its tributary Camp Creek are permanent, but blocked by a series of big rooster-tailing waterfalls that finally plunge directly into the bed of Big Dry.

This section, from the mouth of Spider Creek down to the North Fork, is very lightly traversed and always provides beautiful browns that may never see a fly; there are some very nice holes. Fish this water as you would any other good-sized rushing canyon stream in the Mogollons. A weighted nymph drifted under a rock ledge will produce browns in the 14-inch range, guaranteed to put a nice bend in your rod. No need for a strike indicator—these hungry fish try to pull the rod from your hands. Swifter water requires a few split-shot weights, 2 or 3 inches above the lure. Of course, browns always respond to Mepps-type spinners in the deeper waters, but these are less enjoyable to use.

Spruce Creek

Big Dry's beautiful upper tributary, Spruce Creek, holds browns for 200 to 300 yards below a series of barrier falls, and supports a peculiar relict strain of Gila trout above and within. These fish have very few spots, heavy spotting being the principal distinguishing feature of the Gila trout species. In fact, they more closely resemble Apache trout, most having no discernible redband, no prominent parr marks, and only the faintest bluish sheen. They inhabit about 3 miles of permanent stream tucked between 10,650-foot Black Mountain and other high peaks at the roof of the Mogollon Range. In addition to this stream's namesake spruce forest (which also gives Black Mountain its name) and the aspens and blue grouse on Spruce Creek Saddle, the 7,000-foot streambed is adorned with mountain-loving redstem dogwood, thimbleberries, and even small raspberry thickets, as well as the usual willow growth. May and June mornings are filled with the songs of the hermit thrush, as opposed to the canyon wrens you hear in the lower Big Dry Box.

Spruce Creek is at present closed to fishing. It is not, however, closed to looking. If you can resist the temptation to fish this exponent of all remote and hidden Southwest trout habitats, you may want to put your rod away momentarily and spend an afternoon here. An old miner's cabin has been converted into a fine campspot where the trail leads down to the stream just above the upper falls.

CHAPTER NINE

Blue River

Location: Blue Range Primitive Area, Apache-Sitgreaves National
Forest, Apache and Graham Counties, Arizona; Dry Blue RARE II
roadless area, Gila National Forest, Catron County
Maps: Gila National Forest, Apache-Sitgreaves National Forest
Visitors Maps; Clifton title, USGS 1:100,000 series
Elevation: 3,900–7,000 feet
Length: 75 miles
Best Times: April, May, September-November
Fish Species: brown trout, rainbow trout, Sonoran sucker, desert
sucker, Gila mountain-sucker, speckled dace, loach minnow, channel
catfish
Fishable Tributaries: in New Mexico, Dry Blue Creek, Pace Creek
(trib. to Dry Blue); in Arizona, Campbell Blue Creek, Buckalou
Creek, Castle Creek, Coleman Creek, Cienega Creek (tribs. to
Campbell Blue); Bush Creek; Lamphier Canyon; Foote Creek (two
branches); Grant Creek (plus two tributaries); McKittrick Creek; KP
Creek (plus three tributaries); Raspberry Creek; Strayhorse Creek;
Thomas Creek (plus one tributary); Little Blue Creek, Hannah Creek

The state of Arizona is divided north and south by the relentlessly uplifted
Colorado Plateau. On the uplifted side lie the state's forests, from the
Christmas tree spruce-fir of the Mountain Lying Down, as the Navajo
call the North Kaibab Plateau, to the yellow pine forests of the Mogollon

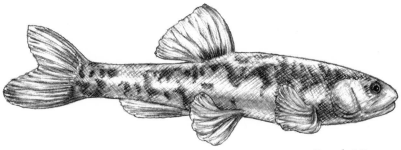

Loach Minnow

Plateau of the Sierra del Gila. The famous Mogollon Rim actually functions as a sort of pushoff for the southern edge of the Colorado Plateau. Below the rim, and beyond lesser nearby breaks in the land, like the Nantac Rim and the Big Lue Mountains, lie the cactus plains and desert mountains for which the state is widely known.

Mountain ranges and rivers are not aware of longitudinal medians, and the eastern boundary of Arizona's Mogollon Rim and Blue Range move seamlessly into the state of New Mexico near the 109th west parallel. The 75-mile-long Blue River, forming on the Mogollon Rim and flowing through the entire length of the Blue Range, is an Arizona stream, but it makes a slight detour out of that state. It starts off in Arizona as Campbell Blue Creek on the flank of Middle Mountain atop the Prieto Plateau, flowing through a seam in the upper Blue Range; then, after entering New Mexico, it acquires the combined flow of two tributaries, Dry Blue and Pace Creeks. Here it becomes the Blue River proper before returning to Arizona, 2 miles below. Blue River drainage holds by my count no fewer than twenty trout-bearing streams, but only three of these flow in New Mexico. To be properly informed of the other seventeen you'll have to wait for the first edition of *Fly-Fishing Arizona.*

The brief section of Campbell Blue Creek in New Mexico holds rainbows, but in most years is not terribly good fishing. The banks are open and grazed, the stream is shallow and exposed to the sun. The Arizona section upstream between Luce Ranch and the Coronado Trail (US 180) provides fairly good fishing for browns, rainbows, and a few hybridized

Apache trout. Federally endangered loach minnows are also present both here and in the Blue River below.

Dry Blue Creek holds browns and is recharged by good springs shortly above its merging with Campbell Blue Creek. Reproduction of these fish is excellent, and water quality here in recent years has been superior to the other branch. In the summer of 1995, Dry Blue had a good current of cold, clean water at its mouth with Campbell Blue, which was dry at that particular spot for a period of weeks. The Blue River itself is formed here, with only fair fishing for a mile or so before the stream returns to Arizona.

Upstream tributary Pace Creek also has a growing population of browns, following a few years of stream improvement by a recently rejuvenated beaver colony and, far more significantly, improved watershed conditions following a rest from cattle grazing. The grazing rest has provided the new growth of willows and cottonwoods that have in turn allowed beaver to stage a comeback here, since beaver and cattle compete for the same plants. The upland watershed within the Gila Forest's Luna Grazing Allotment has been rested for the past few years, and not only the beaver colony but also the entire stream bottom is being recolonized by willows. Browns can now be had in several ponds in Pace just upstream from Dry Blue. Ten years ago there was nothing in this same stream. The sudden reappearance of trout here gives an idea as to the potential for trout habitat elsewhere in the area and in the entire Sierra del Gila.

Few people are aware of the good things that have happened on Pace and Dry Blue Creeks. This is part of the "back forty" of the Luna Ranger District. The whole Dry Blue watershed is at present roadless in New Mexico, and visitation of the area, always slight, is down. The old dirt road from Luna, down to and along the Dry Blue, has been formally closed by the Luna Ranger District, and, more effectively, closed by washouts. *Natura triumphans.* Given the improving natural conditions, the stream should produce progressively better fishing in the near future, or at least until current management policies change. When or how they might is anyone's guess.

CHAPTER TEN

Lakes of the Gila National Forest

Bill Evans Lake

Location: Gila National Forest, private land

Maps: Gila NF Visitors Map; Mogollon title, USGS 1:100,000 series

Elevation: 4,675 feet

Size: 62 acres

Best Times: spring and fall

Fish Species: rainbow trout, largemouth bass, crappie, bluegill, catfish

Bill Evans Lake is a fantastic bass lake that is stocked with rainbow trout from 1 November to 31 March. Its water, owned by the Phelps Dodge Company, is pumped from the Gila River 300 feet below and eventually used for mining operations. As it leaves the river it passes through man-made channels growing an abundance of freshwater shrimp. The exchange of nutrition-rich water, along with the lack of siltation from runoff that most reservoirs receive, makes the lake very productive, resulting in excellent fishing for largemouth bass, crappie, bluegill, and winter-stocked trout. The Department of Game and Fish has a perpetual fishing easement, and free camping is allowed at the lake.

To reach Bill Evans Lake, take US 180 north for 26 miles from Silver City. Turn west on Forest Road 809. Follow FR 809 for 3 miles along the Gila River. Turn left on a gravel road leading up a hill to Bill Evans Lake.

Fly fishers can fish from most of the bank as there is little to obstruct casting. When trout are stocked in the lake, early morning or late evening is best. Exceptionally large bass grow here, including several state records. The riprap along the dam is a good area for both trout and bass. The cattails in the northeast corner harbor bass and bluegill. Boats and flotation devices are allowed, but no gas motors.

The local fishermen usually troll flies from a boat. Popular flies include Woolly Worms (brown or green), Peacock Nymphs, and Pistol Petes. Adams, Renegades, and Rio Grande Kings can be good producers in the spring.

Lake Roberts

Location: Gila National Forest
Maps: Gila NF Visitors Map; Silver City title, USGS 1:100,000 series
Elevation: 6,030 feet
Size: 71 acres
Best Times: fall and spring
Fish Species: rainbow trout

Lake Roberts, a very popular put-and-take trout lake, is an impoundment on Sapillo Creek. To reach it, take NM 15 north from Silver City for 20 miles to NM 35. Follow NM 35 east for 4 miles. This route is not suitable for long trailers. Instead, take the route along the Mimbres Valley, 20 miles east of Silver City. Near San Lorenzo follow NM 61 and NM 35 northeast for 20 miles.

Recently dredged to remove accumulated silt, Lake Roberts is a year-round trout lake dependent on stocked fish. The pH is too high in summer to stock trout, and so it's stocked only in the fall, winter, and spring. Summer fishing is slow because of warm water sending the fish to the bottom or to cold water springs. In summer the surface becomes very mossy.

Trout can be caught by wading the edges and casting flies along the bulrushes. An effective method to catch larger rainbows is to fish with a sinking line deep along the face of the dam. Boats and flotation devices are allowed, but no gas motors. Typical of all Gila lakes, popular flies include Woolly Worms (brown or green), Peacock Nymphs, and Pistol

Petes. Adams, Renegades, and hair-winged Rio Grande Kings can be good producers in the spring and fall. In the winter, small caddis imitations (tan with a black head) work well.

Snow Lake

Location: Gila National Forest
Maps: Gila NF Visitors Map; Mogollon Mountains title, USGS 1:100,000 series; USFS Wilderness Map
Elevation: 7,400 feet
Size: 72 acres
Best Times: spring and fall
Fish Species: rainbow trout

This beautiful remote trout lake located at the northern edge of the Gila Wilderness is a reservoir on Snow Creek, an intermittent tributary of the Middle Fork Gila River. There are three routes to Snow Lake. The best way is to take Forest Road 141 south from Reserve and follow the signs to Snow Lake for 40 miles. The last 18 miles are unpaved. A scenic route is State Road 78 starting 4 miles north of Glenwood, about 30 miles of very slow driving and closed in winter. Don't use this route if you are pulling a long trailer. A third route from the east is to take the Cuchillo Exit from I-25 five miles north of Truth or Consequences. Follow NM 52 west past Winston. Ten miles north of Winston, turn left on NM 59 and go 30 miles to Beaverhead. Follow Forest Route 141 west for 30 miles of unimproved road to Snow Lake.

Snow Lake is stocked with rainbow trout. Many anglers fish with bait from the bank, but flies can be effective here too, especially early and late in the day. Most locations offer plenty of room for a back cast. Try fishing along the riprap at the dam. Boats with electric trolling motors and flotation devices are allowed. There is a concrete boat ramp. Trolling flies can be successful, especially along the dam in spring. Fishing remains almost as good through the summer, picking up again in the fall. In winter its remoteness makes it inaccessible much of the time.

Popular flies include Woolly Worms (brown or green), Peacock Nymphs, and Pistol Petes. Adams, hair-winged Rio Grande Kings, Renegades, and Mosquito patterns can be good producers. For those with a depth finder, fishing the channel with sinking nymphs at the upper end of the lake can be very rewarding. A beautiful fee campground (Dipping Vat Campground) sits on a hilltop overlooking the lake.

Bear Canyon Dam

Location: Gila National Forest
Maps: Gila NF Visitors Map; Silver City title, USGS 1:100,000 series
Elevation: 6,100 feet
Size: 25 acres
Best Times: spring
Fish Species: rainbow trout, bass, channel catfish, bluegill, crappie

Bear Canyon Dam is 2 miles north of the town of Mimbres on NM 61 on a small stream feeding the Mimbres River. The road to the lake from NM 61 is short, steep, and rough. This is a winter trout water, stocked from November to March. It also contains largemouth bass, bluegill, catfish, and crappie. Boats and flotation devices are allowed, but no gas motors.

Wall Lake

Location: Gila National Forest
Maps: Gila NF Visitors Map; Truth or Consequences title, USGS 1:100,000 series
Elevation: 6,550 feet
Size: 15 acres
Best Times: May–June
Fish Species: rainbow trout

Wall Lake, stocked with catchable rainbow trout, is a small impoundment on Taylor Creek in the northeastern part of the Gila National Forest, 6 miles south of Beaverhead. This lake is silting in and is marginal trout habitat. It becomes very mossy in the summer. A beautiful, free camping area is located near the lake.

The best route here is via the Cuchillo Exit from I-25 five miles north of Truth of Consequences. Follow NM 52 for 10 miles past Winston, then turn left on NM 59 and go 30 miles to Beaverhead. At Beaverhead go south on Forest Road 150 for 6 miles to Wall Lake.

Quemado Lake

Location: Apache National Forest
Maps: Gila NF Visitors Map; Quemado title, USGS 1:100,000 series
Elevation: 7,600 ft
Size: 131 acres
Best Times: spring and fall
Fish Species: rainbow trout, grass carp
Contributed by: George Sanders

Quemado Lake is located within a half-hour drive of Highway 60 and the town that gave it its name. The town of Quemado is 104 miles west of Socorro on US 60. The lake is 14 miles south of town on NM 32, then 4 miles east on NM 103.

This is a 131-acre trout lake that grows large trout. An impoundment on Largo Creek, located at 7,600 feet in the northern Gila National forest, Quemado is nestled in piñon-juniper canyons with a deep downside and a relatively shallow upper end. The orientation is slightly northwest to southeast, which presents the wind with a clear shot down the length of the lake. For this reason, float tubers must be aware of their position and watch the weather. A float tube can be launched from any point along the shoreline.

This lake receives moderate fishing pressure during the warm weather months, with small boat trollers from Albuquerque, Gallup, Grants, and Silver City making up a large share of these fishers. There are also a number of private houses, mostly seasonal, in the area below the dam. There you'll find a store, restaurant, and bar, which are quite busy in season. The camping opportunities here are excellent, with new camping facilities on the north promontory and the original campground about one mile beyond the twin inlets in the upper lake.

This lake is located at the northern end of Slaughter Mesa, a trophy-elk hunting area which is very popular in the fall. When the hunters arrive for elk season the fishing pressure has drastically decreased and the fishing is prime.

The stocked rainbow trout grow fast in this lake. In the upper, or southern, end you'll find two major inlets, each extending 50–75 yards back up into the meadow. These inlets have many dead submerged trees and great fishing from float tubes or from the banks, as there are few back-casting hazards. There is also a small island ringed by deep channels that stay relatively weed- and moss-free through the summer months. A favorite method of fly-fishing the upper end is to cruise the channels around this island, casting blind toward the weed-bed margins. Until recently, weed growth was so dense in July and August that negotiating this part of the lake was difficult for boaters and tubers. Grass carp were introduced to help with the vegetation and have made an impact. The carp have reached mammoth size, and some fishermen are targeting these now.

There is a dense growth of tule reeds and cattails along the shoreline in the upper half of the lake. In the lower half of the lake the shore is steeper, though sometimes wooded, which makes fly casting from the shore problematical.

In choosing a fly, a normal selection of lake flies work here. Due to the milfoil and pondweed, you'll find a huge snail population. Leeches, Woolly Burgers, Woolly Worms, Damsel Nymphs, Madam X's, JJ Specials and Double Hackle Peacock Nymphs work well. The damselfly nymphs start moving toward shore in late May and early June. As with other lakes at this elevation, the middle summer months are slow, with the weeds frustrating most float tubers.

The big fish become really active in October and right up until Thanksgiving when you may have to break ice to launch a tube from shore. Be prepared for snow anytime after mid-October.

Part III:
Fly-Fishing the Sacramento and
Zuni Mountains

CHAPTER ELEVEN

Streams of the Sacramento Mountains

Even though many more miles of good trout streams are found in the Gila National Forest, the Sacramento Mountains draw far more fly fishers. Why? Foremost, the streams in the Sacramento Mountains are all near roads. A fly fisher can put on his hip boots at the car and walk to the stream, but in the Gila he often backpacks or horse packs in to fish. Secondly, the Mesilla Valley Flyfishers and Rio Peñasco Fishing Company have leases with ranchers to manage the best 7 miles of trout stream in southern New Mexico for fly fishers. These 7 miles of the Rio Peñasco are known to anglers all over the southwestern United States and beyond. You'll find plenty of other fine trout waters in these blue mountains that rise abruptly from the surrounding desert plains.

Most of the fishing waters listed are on city, Indian Reservation, or private lands located within the general boundaries of the Lincoln National Forest. You can use the Lincoln National Forest map as a guide to the streams in the Sacramentos.

Water conditions can cause dramatic changes in the population of fish in these streams. As in the Gila region, wet years mean better fishing than during dry spells. On any given stream, one year of good fishing may be followed by a season when you'll find almost no fish. Over the years I have seen abundant changes in the trout populations in all of these streams.

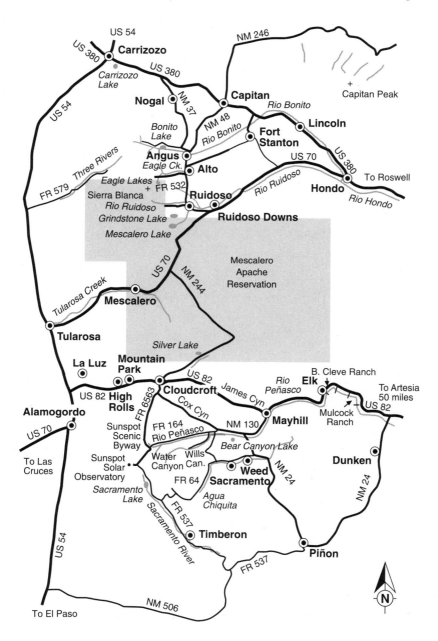

Fly-Fishing in the Sacramento Mountains

Agua Chiquita Creek

Location: Sacramento Mountains, Lincoln National Forest
Maps: Lincoln NF Visitors Map; Alamogordo title, USGS 1:100,000 series
Elevation: 6,000–8,000 feet
Length: 12 miles
Best Times: March–November
Fish Species: brook trout

Agua Chiquita is a very small spring creek in the Sacramento Mountains, 25 miles southeast of Cloudcroft, New Mexico. It averages 1 to 2 feet wide and about 10 inches deep. The high calcium carbonate content of the spring waters entering the creek causes the bottom to consist principally of hardpan. The current is slow and easily waded with hip boots.

To reach the Agua Chiquita go 22 miles southeast from Cloudcroft on Highway 130 and Highway 24 to the town of Weed. At Weed, turn right on Highway 521. Follow Highway 521 for 4 miles to the village of Sacramento where the road changes to Forest Road 64 that parallels the stream to its headwaters. Follow FR 64 until you run out of blacktop. The lower section of stream belonging to the Forest Service is behind you, just past the cattle guard.

There are three stretches of fishable stream, totaling about 5 miles, that are on Forest Service land. Brook trout inhabit the entire stretch of water from the town of Weed up to Sand Springs. A few rainbow trout can be found around the town of Sacramento.

The first half-mile section of stream on Forest Service land is 2 miles from the village of Sacramento. It was overgrazed, is very shallow, and becomes murky when it rains. In the last few years fences have been erected, structures built, and fishing is improving. This area appears in the Sikes Act (Habitat Improvement Stamp) video as an example of the positive changes the act can bring about.

The next section of public water is about 2 miles upstream. Going upstream it starts in a little field and then flows from a small forested canyon that is very close to the road, but gives the impression that you

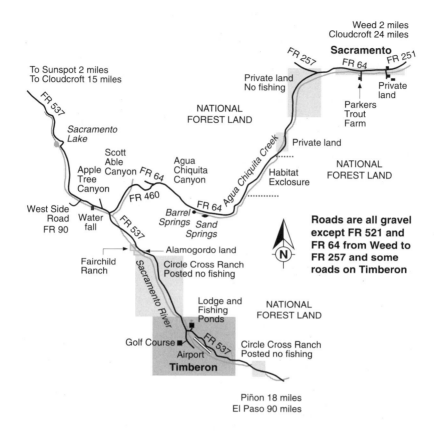

Roads are all gravel
except FR 521 and
FR 64 from Weed to
FR 257 and some
roads on Timberon

Sacramento River and Aqua Chiquita Creek

are in a wilderness. This section of stream has natural logs and holes
as well as structures built by the Forest Service. Upstream from this section, the stream crosses the road onto a ranch for about .7 miles. As
the creek crosses to the west of the road, it returns to Forest Service
land. Above this is the headwater area, a meadow stream with little
cover except for one hard-to-fish area overgrown with willows.

Before the Forest Service started to improve this part of the stream,
it contained few fish. It had steep, somewhat undercut banks with no
hiding or holding places for fish. In 1985, the Forest Service stocked it
with wild transplanted brook trout. When they found that the fish lived
through the winter and spawned, the Forest Service began to place

logs in the stream to improve the habitat. They have placed several hundred structures in the stream. The best part of this section is fenced as a Wildlife Habitat Area, where water plants have grown so well that the stream has become up to 10 feet wide. The stream channel has disappeared and now there are several current channels between areas of vegetation. Now the headwater section stays clear, even following a hard rain.

On very small streams with skittish brook trout, like the Agua Chiquita, it is a good idea to crawl up to a pool and make a kneeling cast. Hold the fly and a loop of leader in your noncasting hand. Give the rod a flip up and back, just enough to get the line airborne, then make a forward cast with no backcast. When the fly is taken by a fish, raise the rod tip slightly to set the hook.

After releasing the fish, move to the next pool and repeat the sequence. Experience has shown me that catching one fish in a small pool will put down the others for a few minutes. If you don't have a strike on the first cast, make one or two more, then move on. When you spook a fish before a cast is made—usually one stationed below the pool—it will run into the pool and put all the fish on alert. The brook trout in Agua Chiquita Creek are wild trout. On a normal day you can expect to catch several 7- to 8-inch brook trout and many smaller fish. If you are lucky, you may hook a brook trout in the 9- to 14-inch range. This stream is overpopulated with small trout. If you want a limit of small fish to eat, do so in good conscience.

Although the brookies are small, they can be fun to catch. It can be a great place to teach youngsters to fly-fish if they have the patience to retrieve their fly when it lands in the grass, as will happen to all but the best fly fishers. Two of my children and I were fishing upstream together and took turns casting to each hole. When my daughter got her fly caught in grass or bushes, she would lay her fly rod down and my son would cast. When he got hung up, I would do the same. Then all of us would walk up, retrieve our flies, and start over on the next hole. We had a good time, and all of us caught fish.

The creek contains caddisflies, mayflies, and midges. There is an abundance of grasshoppers during the summer and fall. Joe's Hopper is an effective pattern in the summer and fall. Elk Hair Caddis are good in spring and summer. In colder weather or off-color water, use nymph patterns or Woolly Worms. I have also had good luck with a Black Deerhair Ant.

Places to stay or camp near the Agua Chiquita include Forest Service and private campgrounds around Cloudcroft or Mayhill, or primitive camping throughout the Lincoln National Forest.

Sacramento River

Location: Sacramento Mountains, Lincoln National Forest
Maps: Lincoln NF Visitors Map; Alamogordo title, USGS 1:100,000 series
Elevation: 6,000–7,500 feet
Length: 12 miles
Best Times: March–November
Fish Species: brook and rainbow trout

The Sacramento River is a small stream in the Sacramento Mountains, 25 miles south of Cloudcroft. Three routes lead to it. From Cloudcroft go south toward Sunspot on NM 130 for 2 miles, then turn right on Forest Road 6563. Follow this winding mountain highway (Sunspot Scenic Byway) for about 14 miles. Just before you get to Sunspot turn left on Forest Road 537. Follow this gravel road for about 7 miles to the intersection of West Side Road (Forest Road 90). The stream is on your right and runs between two marshes. This is the beginning of the fishable area and is on Forest Service land.

From El Paso, Texas, you can take US 54 north past Orogrande (about 50 miles). Then turn east on NM 506 (gravel). Follow the signs to Timberon (a private recreational development) for 45 miles. The third option is to start from Artesia and take US 82 and NM 24 west to Piñon. From Piñon follow Forest Road 537 for 20 miles to Timberon.

The Sacramento is 3 to 4 feet wide and about 6 inches deep. Because of the high calcium carbonate content in the spring waters feeding this stream, most of the bottom is covered with caliche in the upper part of the stream. Farther downstream the bottom is mostly gravel. In the last few years, watercress has taken hold in slow parts of the stream. The current is slow and it is easy to wade with hip boots.

The stream parallels Forest Road 537 from the headwaters to where it ends in the desert. Following the river from the headwaters, which contain brook trout, the first 2 miles from West Side Road past Apple Tree Canyon and Scott Able Canyon to the Fairchild Ranch are very popular for primitive camping (no facilities).

The Forest Service, with help from the National Wild Turkey Federation of Otero County, has installed structures and planted watercress in the upper part of the river. One frequently used camping and picnic area is a waterfall just downstream of the marsh, south of West Side Road. Scott Able Canyon has a small permanent stream that does not have any fish.

The next half-mile of the Sacramento River is on private land and has been open to fishing, but has little fish habitat. Following this section is a quarter-mile stretch that belongs to the city of Alamogordo. This stretch is open to fishing and contains structures placed by the Mesilla Valley Flyfishers. The next 3 miles downstream are on the Circle Cross Ranch and posted.

Just south of the Circle Cross Ranch is Timberon, a private recreational development with about 3 miles of stream kept ungrazed for twenty years. The stream has narrowed and there are many excellent holes. At present, except for one small fenced area, the stream on Timberon is open to the public and is choice fishing.

Rainbow trout lived downstream from Timberon before the fire in 1994 that killed all fish in the lower part of the stream. The brook trout will come back, but it's questionable whether the rainbows will. The final 3 miles of the river have been overgrazed, making it shallow and wide. The Forest Service has used Habitat Stamp money to fence public land here, and the stream is improving. Stream structures were placed in the stream and willows were planted in 1990 and 1991. These last 3 miles have become a popular fishing area.

The brook trout and rainbow trout of the Sacramento River are wild trout. Because brook trout tend to overpopulate and become stunted, the Department of Game and Fish moves some of them to streams where they will have a better chance to grow. These replants are the only fish stocked in the Sacramento River.

The rainbow trout may have come from a washed-out private pond that may have been stocked in the past, but hatchery trout are not stocked by the Department of Game and Fish. On a normal day you can expect to catch several 9- to 10-inch brook trout and many smaller fish, depending on where you are fishing. The trout in the Sacramento River move up and down the stream depending on water conditions, making them hard to find at times. If you are lucky you may hook a 12- to 16-inch brook trout or a 12- to 20-inch rainbow trout.

This small stream has a good population of fair-sized fish, but a large harvest would ruin it. I believe if all fishermen returned most fish and only kept one or two for immediate consumption, this stream could provide good fishing for many anglers. Due to the rainbow trout's low reproductive success some years in the Sacramento River, I believe that all should be returned to the stream at this time.

Much of the Sacramento is in forested areas with some stretches having thistles or tall grass on the banks, which makes casting difficult. Several types of cast are needed for such overgrown waters in southern New Mexico. Often you'll have no room for a back cast and sometimes no overhead room, so you might try a roll cast. At times a sidearm cast is required to reach under trees. Frequently I make a cast where the rod is only raised to about the 12:30 position and the line is raised just off the water, then the rod is punched forward. When this fails, use the bow-and-arrow cast.

Dapping can also be successful when cover is available to the side of the water. For this technique and the others, I prefer a 9-foot rod for the control it gives, although you might prefer a shorter rod.

There are caddisflies, mayflies, midges, and dragonfly nymphs in the stream. I have never seen a mayfly hatch but I have seen spinners.

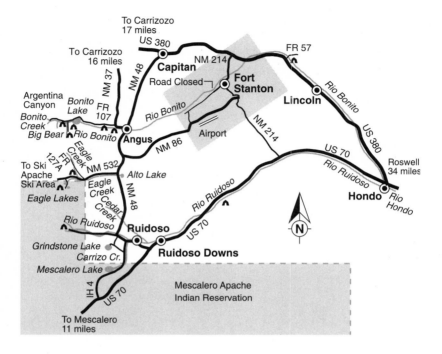

Fly-Fishing the Northern Sacramento Mountains

A survey by the New Mexico Department of the Environment identi-
fied three species of mayflies *Ameletus* (Blue-winged Olive, size 16),
Baetis (Blue-winged Olive, size 16–20), and *Cinygmula* (Blue-winged
Red Quill; use March Brown, size 14–16). They also found two species
of stoneflies—*Amphinemura* (Little Brown, size 12–16) and *Isoperla
perlodidae* (Little Yellow, size 10–12). Caddisflies observed included
Hydropsyche (Spotted Sedge, size 10–16) and *Psychoronia* (Large-cased
Caddis, size 4–10). Other insects found include *Diptera* (true flies—
several species including crane flies), *Coleoptera* (beetles), *Odonata*
(dragonflies), *Mollusca* (snails), and *Annelida* (segmented worms). The
last 3 miles of perennial stream have an abundance of grasshoppers.
Where fast water flows over rocks and logs, black fly larva (*Simulidae*)
and a species of midge (*Diptera*) make the structure look as if it is covered by a dark moss.

Joe's Hopper is an effective pattern in summer and fall. Elk Hair Caddis is good in spring and summer. A size 16 Elk Hair Caddis is a good match for all the stoneflies and caddisflies listed above. You may wish to try an olive Elk Hair Caddis. Mayfly patterns in size 16 will cover all mayflies in this stream. In colder weather or when the water is off-color use nymph patterns or Woolly Worms. I have had terrific luck with Gary Borger's Hair Leg Woolly Worm. The stream gets murky, but it clears up quickly after summer rains. The lower end is fishable all winter.

Places to stay or camp near the Sacramento River include Forest Service and private campgrounds around Cloudcroft, or primitive camping throughout the Lincoln National Forest. There is also a campground, a small store with gas pumps, a motel, and a restaurant at the golf course on Timberon, all open to the public. The area from Apple Tree Canyon to the Fairchild Ranch is my wife's favorite camping spot.

Bonito Creek (Rio Bonito)

Location: Sacramento Mountains, Lincoln National Forest
Maps: Lincoln NF Visitors Map; Ruidoso and Carrizozo titles, USGS 1:100,000 series
Elevation: 6,000–9,000 feet
Length: 25 miles
Best Times: March–May and September–November
Fish Species: brook trout, rainbow trout, brown trout

Rio Bonito (Pretty River) is a small freestone stream originating on the eastern slope of Sierra Blanca Mountain in the Sacramento Mountains, 10 miles north of Ruidoso. It flows east for 25 miles to its confluence with the Rio Ruidoso, where they form the Rio Hondo. It averages 4 to 5 feet wide and about 6 inches deep above Bonito Lake, and, below Fort Stanton, over 12 feet wide and a foot deep. Its bottom consists principally of rocks and sand. Current is usually slow, except during spring runoff, and easily waded with hip boots. The rocky bottom in the headwaters can be slick, so boots with felt soles are recommended.

Bonito Creek is subject to flooding and, in recent years, floods have damaged the streambed. Because of the flood damage and water removal by the city of Alamogordo, the only dependable running water during low water conditions is in the wilderness area and below Fort Stanton. In dry years, the stretch from the wilderness boundary downstream to the lower end of Fort Stanton contains water only in holes and for short stretches below springs.

At times I am amazed at the ability of the fish to return when water conditions improve. Even during normal years, the stream can become low enough to make summer fishing very difficult until the summer rains come. When conditions are good, the Rio Bonito grows large numbers of trout to 14 inches in length, with some even larger.

To reach Rio Bonito, go 8 miles north from Ruidoso on NM 48 until you cross the creek. From the bridge, most of the creek upstream is open to fishing. The stream lies south of and parallel to NM 37 for about 1.5 miles and west along Forest Road 107 for 8 miles to the White Mountain Wilderness boundary. Bonito Lake is about 5 miles upstream from where NM 37 crosses the creek. The other stretch of water that has trout and is open to fishing, when conditions are right, flows through Fort Stanton. Private posted land intermingles with open areas along this river. All of the stream above Bonito Lake is on land belonging to the city of Alamogordo or to the Forest Service, except for a small strip belonging to an outfitter.

One mile above Bonito Lake, the South Fork joins the main stream. Both the main stream and South Fork above Bonito Lake contain a population of small, wild-spawned brook and rainbow trout. The South Fork has 4 miles of good fly-fishing water within the White Mountain Wilderness containing many pools with rainbows and brook trout up to 11 inches. To fish the South Fork, park in the South Fork Campground and take Forest Trail 19. To fish the wilderness portion of the main stream or Argentina Canyon, park at the end of Forest Road 107 and follow Forest Trail 36 or 39. The creek at both parking areas may be dry, but water and fish will be found about one quarter-mile upstream. The main stream also contains some planted rainbow trout whenever there is enough water to merit stocking.

Rio Peñasco below Elk

From the wilderness area downstream to Bonito Lake, the South Fork has flooded frequently since 1976 and has changed its channel several times. Livestock grazing of the stream banks ceased in 1986. With luck, the channel will stabilize and the entire stream will again become productive. In some years during October and November, hundreds of brook trout migrate upstream from Bonito Lake to spawn. Rainbow trout make their run in March and April. I hope that all anglers understand that over-harvesting of these fish will be detrimental to future fishing in this stream.

If you would like to get away from the crowd on a weekend, especially a long weekend, and would like to catch fish by yourself, no matter how small, try Argentina Canyon or the main Bonito Creek in the wilderness. The fish are small, but most people stay on the trails away from the creeks. The South Fork has more and larger fish, but it is almost like a highway with people walking along it. Tributaries like Big Bear Creek and Little Bear Canyon have a few small brook trout.

The city of Alamogordo controls the flow in the stream below Bonito Lake Dam. Most of the stream from Bonito Lake to NM 37 is open to fishing. Alamogordo owns most of the land in this area. The remainder of the land is private, with a few posted areas. When there is enough water, this sector is stocked with rainbows. At times it also contains a large population of brook trout. In some years fifty fish a day were caught and released during the spring.

Bonito Creek flows for 7 miles across Fort Stanton reservation where it is managed by the Bureau of Land Management. In this area the streambed is mostly sand. Much of it can dry up in arid years, but the upper section has good holes that hold fish and the lower end has a dependable spring.

As this is being written the Bureau of Land Management is negotiating a land exchange for the area downstream from Fort Stanton. This stretch has dependable water from the springs on Fort Stanton and downstream. The Mesilla Valley Flyfishers and Bureau of Land Management placed large boulders in a portion of the stream on Fort Stanton in 1993. Grazing practices are changing to protect the riparian areas, and fishing should improve in the future. The Department of Game and Fish began stocking Fort Stanton in 1993.

The brook and brown trout in Bonito Creek are wild. Rainbows are stocked but there are also wild reproducing rainbows above Bonito Lake and downstream from Fort Stanton. The wild rainbows have some cutthroat crossbreeding, some with marks on the throat and orange areas on the belly. Brown trout appear in the lower part of the stream.

The food supply is abundant, consisting of caddisflies, mayflies, midges, scuds, water bugs, beetles, and stoneflies. Mixed hatches of mayflies, caddisflies, and Little Yellow Stonefly (size 12) are common in the spring. The South Fork of Bonito has a large dark stonefly that is over an inch in length. Elk Hair Caddis and Renegades are good in spring and summer. Try a yellow Elk Hair Caddis, Light Cahill, or a tan Wulff in the water below Bonito Lake during the spring season. In colder weather, or off-color water, try nymph patterns, Double Hackle Peacocks, or Woolly Worms.

Forest Service, city of Alamogordo, and private campgrounds are located around Bonito Lake and alongside Bonito Creek. Primitive camping is available along the stream 2 miles above Bonito Lake and throughout the Lincoln National Forest.

Ruidoso River (Rio Ruidoso) and Carrizo Creek

Location: Sacramento Mountains, Lincoln National Forest
Maps: Lincoln NF Visitors Map; Ruidoso title, USGS 1:100,000 series
Elevation: 5,000–10,000 feet
Length: 35 miles
Best Times: March–November
Fish Species: rainbow trout and brown trout

Rio Ruidoso is a small freestone river originating on the southern slope of 12,000-foot Sierra Blanca, 10 miles west of Ruidoso, New Mexico. It starts as three forks joining together on the Mescalero Apache Indian Reservation, then flows through the city of Ruidoso east to its confluence with the Rio Bonito, where the Rio Hondo is formed. From the city of Ruidoso downstream, the stream averages 20 feet in width and about 1 foot in depth, with the bottom consisting principally of rocks and sand. Current flow is usually slow and easily waded with hip boots. The rocky bottom in the headwaters can be slick, so boots with felt soles are recommended. The Rio Ruidoso is subject to flooding and can be unfishable during spring runoff and after heavy rains.

To reach the upper Rio Ruidoso on the Mescalero Reservation, drive west on Sudderth Drive in Ruidoso to Main Road (upper canyon). Follow Main Road for about 2 miles to a gate in the road. Just beyond the gate is a small building where camping and fishing permits are sold. The cost for fishing on the Mescalero Apache Indian Reservation is $4 per day for a 12-fish limit.

The river is a series of pools with sharp drops where the water flows over a few rocks into the next pool. This part of the river has brown trout and rainbow trout. It is open for fishing from the middle of May to the middle of September. Rainbows are stocked throughout the summer, but anglers will find the browns more sporting on flies. The rainbows are all 9-to-10-inch stocked fish. The browns are usually smaller wild fish with a few bigger ones in the large pools.

All the river east of the reservation is on private land or Ruidoso city land, but the 7 miles through the city of Ruidoso are, by tradition, open to fishing. The Rio Ruidoso runs along Main Road in the upper canyon, crossing it twice. From the traffic circle east, it runs on the north side of Sudderth Drive to the intersection of us 70. It continues on the north side of the highway past the town of Ruidoso Downs. In Ruidoso the gradient becomes less and the river has pools interspersed by riffles. There are some areas that are channeled and riprapped. Access can be found at Two Rivers Park or at most of the street crossings throughout the city of Ruidoso. Fishermen must respect private property by not parking in driveways and not crossing posted land.

In this area NMG&F stocks the river with 9- to 11-inch rainbows and brown trout fry. After rains or nearby construction work this section of the river can be muddy and unfishable. If it is, check the upper canyon and below where Carrizo Creek enters the river, or Carrizo Creek itself. They may be clearer, depending on the source of the mud.

Carrizo Creek runs from Mescalero Lake to Two Rivers Park where it joins the Rio Ruidoso. The 2-mile section from Carrizo Lodge, on Carrizo Creek Road, to the confluence with the Rio Ruidoso is a good, small tailwater with many brown trout. Most of the browns in this creek are 10 to 12 inches.

The area below the city of Ruidoso is posted ranch land, yet if asked, most owners will give permission to fish. In most of this area the pools are mixed with long riffles; most of the fish are browns. Some of these holes have a good population of 12- to 15-inch fish with a few much larger. In 1993, a half-mile of private water was opened to fishermen as a Special Trout Water. This section is located between Ruidoso and Ruidoso Downs in the Hollywood area. The rules stipulate lures with single barbless hooks and a two-fish limit.

The brown trout in the Rio Ruidoso are wild, either stream spawned or stocked as fry. The rainbow trout are stocked. The food supply is abundant, consisting of caddisflies, mayflies, midges, scuds, and stoneflies. Mixed hatches of mayflies, caddisflies, and a Little Yellow Stonefly are common in the spring. Gold-ribbed Hare's Ear and Renegades are good twelve months of the year. Elk Hair Caddis and Wulff patterns are good spring through fall. Attractor patterns are good on the reservation in the small choppy water there, but in Ruidoso and below, matching the hatch becomes more important.

Places to stay or camp near the Rio Ruidoso include the Mescalero Apache Indian Reservation Campground and private campgrounds in Ruidoso and along the Ruidoso River east of town. Motels abound in Ruidoso. The Mesilla Valley Flyfishers (P. O. Box 2222, Las Cruces, New Mexico, 88004) has obtained a lease on the Hurd Ranch located at San Patricio, New Mexico, 20 miles east of Ruidoso. The cost to fish this water is membership ($20/year) and a daily permit ($10/day). The Hurd Ranch has about 2 miles of the Ruidoso River.

Peñasco River (Rio Peñasco)
Location: Sacramento Mountains, Lincoln National Forest
Maps: Lincoln NF Visitors Map; Alamogordo title, USGS 1:100,000 series
Elevation: 5,300–8,800 feet
Length: 40 miles
Best Times: March–November
Fish Species: rainbows, and brown trout

I heard stories about the big fish in this river long before I fished it. One example was a fisherman telling about stopping at a bridge and catching a 24-inch rainbow on the first cast. Later on I did fish this area, but have never had any luck. The river on both sides of this bridge is on Forest Service land but only for a short distance. However, I have participated in an electrofishing survey with fisheries students from New Mexico State University just a little way downstream, on private land. In this area the Rio Peñasco looks to be about 2 feet wide, and a 24-inch fish had better be careful where it turns around. When we did the survey, we put the probes (about a 1-foot ring) against the banks, and they disappeared under the banks. When the shocker was turned on many fish floated out from under the banks. One measured over 19 inches, big enough for any honest fisherman to call it a 2-foot fish. The headwaters of the Rio Peñasco originate in a marsh along Forest Road 6563 (Sunspot Scenic Byway) about 10 miles south of Cloudcroft. The river flows east paralleling Forest Road 164 (gravel) for 11 miles, picking up water from Water and Wills Canyons. Then it parallels NM 130 for 9 miles to Mayhill. The remainder of the Peñasco's trout water parallels NM 82 for 20 miles to the Dunken Bridge.

In dry years, the river will dry up at Elk, and if Peñasco were a normal desert stream, this would be the end of the fishing. About a mile below Elk, however, the real Rio Peñasco springs to life. In just a few hundred yards this river can go from no water to a strong flow 20 feet wide and 2 feet deep. Except during floods, most of the water in the last 10 miles is from the springs and is by far the best trout habitat in this part of New Mexico. This section of the Rio Peñasco sees as many fly fishers as all the rest of the streams in southern New Mexico put together.

The river from the headwaters to Elk is for the most part channelized and is essentially a long run. The upper part of the river expands slowly from being quite small to about 8 feet in width and 2.5 feet deep; it tends to be murky with a muddy bottom. This section has little vegetation growing in the water, but does have undercut banks to

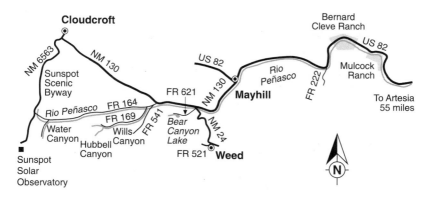

Rio Peñasco

provide deeper holes. Below Elk, where the river widens, the bottom is sand, gravel, and rocks, with vegetation growing in the flats. In this spring creek section the water is usually very clear.

The Rio Peñasco is all on private land, except about 5 miles in the headwaters belonging to the Forest Service, with very few fish. At present there is no shade or fish cover on the upper part of the river, and water temperatures increase to dangerous levels in summer. With the advent of the Habitat Improvement Stamp, this is changing. The Forest Service has completed some stream improvements, and brown trout fry have been planted in this area, but they have disappeared. Some rainbow trout are also in this section of the river during cool weather.

The balance of the river contains a large population of brown trout and some rainbow trout, but fishing here requires landowner permission. The best fly-fishing area, and the best fishing I have had on this river, has been below Elk, but I have caught a few trout at points throughout the Rio Peñasco. They have all been very fat!

For several years before September 1997, the Mesilla Valley Flyfishers had agreements with two ranches on the river downstream from Elk, making sections of the river available to members of fly-fishing clubs at a nominal fee ($10 per day). As of September 1997, the Mulcock Ranch has become a private fishing club. For information on fishing the Mulcock Ranch, contact Charles Mulcock (Mayhill, NM) at the ranch, located between mile markers 50 and 51 on NM 82. The Mesilla Valley Flyfishers still have a lease with the Bernard Cleve Ranch and, as this book is being written, are looking to lease more water on the Rio Peñasco.

The club stocks the river with rainbow trout and brown trout, as additions to the wild browns. Only artificial flies and lures with a single barbless hook are permitted. The daily limit on the Cleve Ranch is one rainbow over 20 inches. The river on the Bernard Cleve Ranch (1.5 miles of river) runs parallel to NM 82 between mile markers 47 and 49. See the map for ranch locations. The section of river between these two ranches is leased by the Rio Peñasco Fishing Company and is only available for fishing with a paid guide.

In addition to the Peñasco's wild (stream-born or fry-planted) browns and stocked rainbows, there is a fall spawning population that appear to be cutbows, successfully reproducing upstream from Mayhill. Most of these fish look very much like rainbows, but many of them have two red slash marks on the underside of the lower jaw.

The food supply is abundant, consisting of stoneflies, caddisflies, mayflies, and midges. Biotic inventories performed by the New Mexico Department of Game and Fish and the New Mexico Environmental Improvement Division have found: stoneflies, *Isoperla* (Little Yellow Stonefly, size 10–16) and *Nemouridae* (Little Brown Stonefly, size 12–16); mayflies, *Baetis* (Blue-winged Olive, size 16–20); *Tricorythodes* (Trico, size 20–22); *Cinygmula* (Blue-winged Red Quill, use March Brown, size 14–16); *Ameletus* and caddisflies, *Rhycophila* (Green Caddis, size 10–16); *Glossosoma* (Turtle Case Maker, size 14–18); *Hydropsyche* (Spotted Sedge, Net Maker, size 10–16); and *Limnephilidae* (Large Case Maker, size 4–10). Many species of true flies are also found in the river, including crane flies and blackflies. Damselflies, aquatic moths, aquatic worms, flatworms, and beetles are found in the river. Below Mayhill the stream also contains a good population of Rio Grande chubs (*Gila pandora*).

Manuel Monasterio, owner of The Reel Life, an Orvis shop in Albuquerque, gives the following advice on flies to use on the Rio Peñasco.

Effective Fly Patterns for the Rio Peñasco
Manuel Monasterio, owner, The Reel Life, an Albuquerque Orvis shop

Many of the fly patterns that are successful on other spring creeks in the West work quite well on the Peñasco. There is just one catch: on the Peñasco they seem to work better for longer periods of time, thanks to the consistently wonderful weather one encounters in this part of the state. One other major difference is that, unlike other spring creeks, the Peñasco doesn't force the angler to "match the hatch" in order to catch fish, though it certainly helps the experienced angler make the most of his or her day.

Mayflies

Baetis hatches are quite significant on the river throughout the year and can successfully be imitated with Pheasant Tail Nymphs in sizes 16–20, and Blue-winged Olives (16–20), tied parachute style. Also good is the olive or gray Comparadun. Hare's Ear Nymphs (14–18) and Parachute Adams(16–18) are also very effective throughout the year.

Tiny tricos begin showing up on the river early in the mornings from March through September. Sparkle Wing Tricos (20–22), as well as Palomino Midges and even Parachute Adams (20–22), fished dry or in the film, will often prove very effective.

Caddisflies

The Peñasco has too many species of caddisflies to mention in this section. All the angler needs to worry about is that they are a significant source of food for the trout, and they are consumed primarily at the immature stage. Norm Mabie of Las Cruces ties a beadhead caddis larvae pattern in tan and olive (14–18), which imitates the different types of free-living caddis. This is easily my favorite nymph for fishing on this river. Prince Nymphs (12–18) and Zug Bugs (12–18) in regular or beadhead are also good imitations for the case-building variety, and all of these patterns are effective year-round.

Adults show up in the summer, at which time the Lafontaine Sparkle Pupa Emerger (14–16) in chartreuse is a good choice, as is Mabie's Diving Caddis (14–16). Other adults can be imitated with Elk Hair Caddis ranging in size from 14 to 20 and in the following colors: light cahill, cinnamon, charcoal gray, and tan.

Terrestrials

This section may as well be retitled "grasshoppers," for this form of terrestrial insect is by far the most productive for the fly fisherman to imitate. Another nice thing about grasshoppers on this river is that they appear in June and last until November, and sometimes later! Dave's Hoppers or similar patterns with legs work very well, as will Madame X, Drowned Hopper, and Yellow or Double Humpy (all in sizes 10–14). CDC Ants (16–18) work throughout the year, and Foam Beetles (14–16) are effective in June and July.

Other Patterns

Midges are available to the trout all year and are a significant part of the trout's diet during the winter months. Mabie's Sidewinder Midge, Palomino Midges, and green Disco Midges (all in 20–22) are good for the immature nymph stage, while Griffith's Gnats and Midge Clusters (both in 16–20) are effective imitations of groups of adults floating on the surface.

Scuds are in the river all year and can be imitated with a light ginger pattern in size 16. Damselflies are also common and can be successfully duplicated with an olive Marabou Damsel nymph in size 12, or a Blue Damsel adult in the same size. The few stoneflies in the river can be matched with a Kauffman Brown Stone in size 12–14 for the nymphs (all year) and a yellow Kauffman Stimulator in size 14 for the adults, which hatch primarily in the winter.

Effective streamers include the JJ Special (Jack Dennis), Bunny Leeches (white, purple, black, olive), Royal Coachman Wet, and Woolly Buggers (black, olive krystal). I would stick to sizes 6–12 on most of these.

Much of this stream can be fished year-round. The portion of the stream along Forest Road 164 can be snowed in during the winter, but the stream below Cox Canyon parallels all-weather roads. This stream has many large fish (over 18 inches) due to good food sources and low fishing pressure. The low fishing pressure is due to limited access because it is on private land.

In the past I have been less successful upstream from Elk and believed there were few fish in the channeled areas. Recent electrofishing with Paul Turner, a fisheries biologist at New Mexico State University, has shown that there is a large population of browns throughout most of this stream and a good population of rainbows in some parts.

Places to stay or camp near the Rio Peñasco include a private campground in Mayhill and several private and National Forest campgrounds between Cloudcroft and Mayhill along NM 82. There are many motels in Cloudcroft, while primitive camping is available in the Lincoln National Forest, especially along the Rio Peñasco headwaters. Bernard Cleve has a campground on his ranch near Elk.

Other fishing streams

Eagle Creek flows off the Mescalero Reservation into the Lincoln National Forest along the road (NM 523) to Ski Apache. It's a very small stream. Its North Fork parallels Forest Road 127A for about 2.5 miles, but is dry much of the year. Upstream, at the end of FR 127A, it becomes perennial and has many small brook and rainbow trout. To fish this stream, one must park before the last few cabins and walk past them. Forest Trail 77 follows the stream for more than a mile. There are several old log structures that have developed large pools, and these are full of trout. The South Fork exits the reservation just downstream from Eagle Lake, running along NM 523 for about a mile before being "dewatered," and holds brook trout and a few rainbows that escape Eagle Lake.

Tularosa Creek, holding stocked rainbows and wild browns, forms on the west slope of the Sacramentos and flows from the Mescalero

Indian Reservation west to Tularosa. The part on the Mescalero Reservation is not open to public. The other part is all private, but most is not posted. Some good browns do come downriver. On the east slope, Cedar Creek has brown trout in Ruidoso. Fresnal Canyon has some trout on private land. Three Rivers has small brook trout from the Three Rivers Campground upstream to the headwaters, about 3 miles.

In the Capitan Mountains, Copeland Creek has a few brook trout in pools upstream from the end of Forest Road 163. There are so few trout in this stream that harvesting any should be a crime. Pine Lodge Creek has brook trout. Arroyo Seco Creek, Michallas Canyon, and Las Tablas Canyon, all in the Capitans, plus Wills Canyon, Hubbell Canyon, Water Canyon, and Silver Springs Canyon, in the Sacramentos, have some potential.

CHAPTER TWELVE

Lakes of the Sacramento Mountains

Richard Ramsey and Ron Smorynski

Alto Lake

Location: Lincoln National Forest
Maps: Lincoln NF Visitors Map; Ruidoso title, USGS 1:100,000 series
Elevation: 7,200 feet
Size: 20 acres
Best Times: spring through fall
Fish Species: rainbow and brook trout

A water source for the city of Ruidoso, Alto Lake is located near Alto village, 5 miles north of Ruidoso on the east side of NM 48. Eagle Creek runs through the lake. Open year-round between 6 A.M. and 10 P.M., with heavy fishing pressure during summer months, it has high banks, making fly-casting difficult.

Rainbow trout are stocked here, and occasionally a few brook trout migrate from Eagle Creek. No boats are allowed, and the posted portion near the outlet is closed to fishing. Crawfish and minnows are prevalent, providing the main forage. On occasion a heavy, late evening mayfly hatch occurs.

There is no camping at Alto Lake. Nearby campgrounds include Oak Grove, Cedar Creek, Skyline, and primitive camping along Forest Road 127A in Lincoln National Forest. There is a campground near Eagle Lake on the Mescalero Apache Indian Reservation. Motels abound in Ruidoso.

Bonito Lake

Location: Lincoln National Forest

Maps: Lincoln NF Visitors Map; Ruidoso title, USGS 1:100,000 series

Elevation: 7,300 feet

Size: 60 acres

Best Times: spring and fall

Fish Species: rainbow and brook trout, carp

Bonito Lake is 12 miles northwest of Ruidoso. To get there take NM 48 north from Ruidoso to NM 37 at Angus. Turn left on NM 37 for one mile, then turn left onto Forest Road 107 (County C-9). Follow FR 107 for 3 miles to Bonito Lake. Bonito Lake is a water supply for the city of Alamogordo.

This is one of the most heavily stocked lakes in the state, with very high use by bait fishermen. Most of the access is a steep bank down to the lake. Only at the Bonito Creek inlet, and the end of one arm, is there room for back casts. Flies can be very effective before the sun hits water in the morning and in the evening at the upper end. Some years it is good for brook trout in October and November, which gather at the inlet before making their spawning run. Wading is not feasible. The lake is open for fishing from 1 April through 30 November, from 6 A.M. to 10 P.M. The posted area at the dam is closed to fishing.

Rainbow trout are stocked, and in some years a few reproduce in Bonito Creek. The lake also contains brook trout and a heavy population of carp. The brook trout spawn in the creek, and numbers are dependent on water flows.

Camping is available at the lake. The city of Alamogordo manages the lake and camping sites, which include West Lake Campground, Kraut Canyon, the apple orchard, and others along the stream, downstream from the dam. South Fork Campground (Forest Service) is a quarter-mile south of West Lake Campground. None of these campgrounds has hook ups. Motels can be found in Ruidoso or Capitan.

Grindstone Lake

Location: Ruidoso, New Mexico

Maps: Lincoln NF Visitors Map; Ruidoso title, USGS 1:100,000 series

Elevation: 7,300 feet

Size: 30 acres

Best Times: spring and fall

Fish Species: rainbow and brown trout

Recently built, heavily fished Grindstone Lake is in Ruidoso near Carrizo Creek. Grindstone's water is piped from the Ruidoso River and is very clear and deep, up to 137 feet. It is stocked with rainbows by the Department of Game and Fish. Some browns come through the pipe from the Ruidoso River. Fishing with flies was very good in the spring of 1991, with room to cast. Nonmotorized boats or float tubes are allowed with a city permit ($5/day). Most of the shore is too steep for wading. There is easy access all around the lake, but only a small parking area. There is no camping at the lake, but there are many hotels and campgrounds around Ruidoso.

Mescalero Lake

Location: Mescalero Apache Indian Reservation

Maps: Lincoln NF Visitors Map; Ruidoso title, USGS 1:100,000 series

Elevation: 7,100 feet

Size: 90 acres

Best Times: spring and fall

Fish Species: cutthroat, rainbow, brown trout

Mescalero Lake on Carrizo Creek at Inn of the Mountain Gods has some large cutthroat and rainbows. To get there from Ruidoso, take Carrizo Creek Road south for 2 miles. From Tularosa, take US 70 east and turn left at the sign for Inn of the Mountain Gods. The lake is heavily stocked with rainbows. It is open year-round with a daily fishing fee ($9/day). Boat rentals are available, but no private boats or float tubes are permitted. The limit is 12 fish per day.

The Inn of the Mountain Gods is an exclusive hotel. There are no campgrounds near the lake. If you don't stay at the Inn look for accommodations in Ruidoso.

Eagle Lakes

Location: Mescalero Apache Indian Reservation
Maps: Lincoln NF Visitors Map; Ruidoso title, USGS 1:100,000 series
Elevation: 7,300 feet
Size: 1.5 acres, each lake
Best Times: summer
Fish Species: rainbow trout

Eagle Lakes, on the Mescalero Apache Indian Reservation, are located 4 miles east of Alto, just off Ski Run Road (Forest Road 107). The lakes are on the South Fork of Eagle Creek. The lower lake has cattails around the lake and moss in the lake. The upper lake has moss and is muddy along the shore. The lakes are open from about 10 May to Labor Day. A tribal permit is required at $4 per day, with a 12-fish limit. Rainbows are stocked every Thursday. These are good fly-fishing ponds, but are heavily fished by bait fishermen. No wading is allowed. There is a tribal campground a short distance from the lakes and primitive camping along the North Fork of Eagle Creek. See Alto Lake for a list of other campgrounds.

Silver Lake

Location: Mescalero Apache Indian Reservation
Maps: Lincoln NF Visitors Map; Ruidoso title, USGS 1:100,000 series
Elevation: 8,000 feet
Size: 5.5 acres
Best Times: summer
Fish Species: rainbow trout
Silver Lake is 9 miles northwest of Cloudcroft on NM 244. This small lake is crowded. It can be fly-fished, but long, light tippets are needed. At times several hatches occur daily. Rainbows are stocked every

Thursday and there are a few carp. There is easy access around the lake, with ample parking. A $4 per day tribal fishing permit is required with a limit of 12 fish per day. The lake is open from mid-May to mid-September.

This lake is within a tribal campground. There are Forest Service campgrounds (Silver, Saddle, and Apache) a few miles away, and Cloudcroft has several motels and restaurants.

Bear Canyon Lake is a very small lake stocked in winter with rainbows. It has some bluegills. At times there is ice fishing at this lake. There is only primitive camping near this pound.

Carrizozo Lake is a small lake near Carrizozo that is stocked in the winter.

Private Lakes

In the Sacramento Mountains there are several private lakes (ponds) where one pays, by the inch, for all fish caught. A state fishing license is not required at these lakes since all of the fish here are stocked by the owner. Most come from Parker Trout Farm, located near Sacramento, New Mexico. These lakes make excellent places to take children and inexperienced fishermen to get some fish to cook over a camp fire.

CHAPTER THIRTEEN

Waters of the Zuni Mountains

Bluewater Creek

Location: Zuni Mountains, Cibola National Forest

Maps: Cibola NF Visitors Map, Zuni/Mt. Taylor Ranger Districts; Zuni title, USGS 1:100,000 series

Elevation: 7,500–8,500 feet

Length: 6 miles

Best Times: spring and fall

Fish Species: rainbow and brown trout

Contributed by: Bill Zeedyk

Trout streams in west-central New Mexico are scarce. One of the few is Bluewater Creek, which flows into the south arm of Bluewater Reservoir, southeast of Thoreau. Fishable length is about 6 miles, most of which is in Cibola National Forest, with the remainder on privately owned or reservation land. Newcomers to Bluewater Creek would do well to pick up a recreation map of Cibola National Forest, Mount Taylor Ranger District, as a guide to road system and land owner-ship patterns.

To reach Bluewater Creek, exit I-40 at Thoreau and take NM 612 through South Bluewater village until the pavement ends. Here the road becomes Forest Road 178, a high-standard, two-lane, all-weather gravel road, which parallels Bluewater Creek for about 2 miles, crossing it once. It's a good route for recreational vehicles.

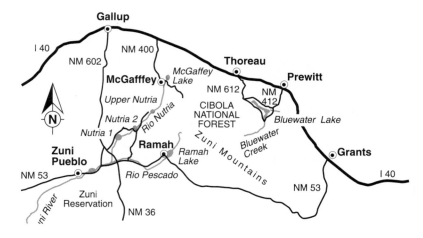

Zuni Mountains

An alternate route is to take NM 122 west from Milan (I-40 Exit 78) for 2 miles. Turn south past the Highway Maintenance Yard and cross over the interstate on Forest Road 180. Follow FR 180 for 13 miles and turn right (north), or take Forest Road 178 about 2 miles to the creek. Forest Road 180 is a single-lane, gravel-surfaced road with heavy log-truck traffic. Be careful! It is not recommended for RVs.

The reach above Andrews Cabin is accessible via a low-standard, primitive ranch road, recommended for 4x4 and high-clearance pick-ups only. From the junction of Forest Roads 180 and 178, take 178 south. Turn right on the first road west. Keep right at the first intersection. It will eventually deliver you to the large meadows paralleling the creek. Park and walk.

The tailwater below the dam also provides some excellent stream fishing in good years for the extent of the irrigation season. This small tailwater is worthy of attention, with some very deep pools and sup-plemental spring water from the canyon walls. It has populations of small browns and some rainbows. This section of stream, called the Rio San Jose, has given up a 5-pound brown and other large resident holdovers. The area within one mile of the dam has great caddis and mayfly hatches for the dry-fly enthusiast.

Blue Water Creek

Bluewater Creek is not stocked, but the lake receives regular plantings of rainbows. Spawning rainbow trout coming up from the lake are
the featured attraction. The run begins in March and is finished by early
May. Usually a few holdover spawners remain through the summer months,
and a growing population of stream-reared fish is present all year.

Bluewater Creek above the lake is a conservation success story. A
decade ago it was a virtual ditch, with few fish and even fewer aes-
thetically redeeming features. However, with some tender loving care
in the form of livestock, off-road vehicle, and recreation controls, it has
recovered and is on the way to being a productive fishery in a very
scenic setting. The riparian zone is green and healthy again, the pools
deeper, the banks stable, and the gravel clean.

This section above the lake can be divided into five distinct reaches
as characterized by stream type, fishability, and accessibility.

The most accessible reach, about 2 miles, parallels Forest Road 178 from
the bridge downstream to the box canyon. It is mostly riffles with a few
deep pools. This reach gets hammered by the bait fishermen during the
spawning run and holds few catchable-sized fish the rest of the year.

Through the box are two distinct reaches. The upper reach is in the National Forest and is excluded from grazing and vehicles. Accessible only on foot, it has many deep pools and some beaver ponds. It carries some holdover spawners and grows stream-reared trout up to 10 or 12 inches. Downstream from the Forest Service boundary fence the creek flows through a heavily overgrazed section before entering the lake. This reach provides good fishing during the run, otherwise nothing. Ownership is a mixture of private and reservation land.

Upstream from the bridge there is a mile-long reach inhabited by a booming beaver colony, lots of willows, deep pools and slack water. It is not grazed, provides excellent fishing during the spring run, and carries some nice stream-reared fish and a few holdovers through the summer. It is chock-full of fingerlings and subadults from 6 to 8 inches long.

Finally, above the fence at Andrews Cabin there is a long reach of low-quality water that carries spawners during the spring, but otherwise few fish. This reach is trapped in the bottom of a 20-foot gully, is overgrazed, and not very attractive. Ownership is a mixture of National Forest and private land.

Anglers will do well to fish the spring run using a black Woolly Bugger. The creek and the lake are full of crayfish and a Woolly Bugger must remind trout of a crawdad. During the summer months you can rely on grasshopper or stonefly patterns. Many terrestrial insects blunder into the water, so almost any dry fly appropriate to the prevailing light conditions will work.

Fly fishermen will find much of Bluewater Creek difficult to fish. Your approach, stealthy not clumsy, is more important than your fly, especially in the willow patches where the ground quakes and trembles underfoot or on gravel bars where the grating of stones underfoot can send trout scurrying.

There are no improved Forest Service campgrounds along Bluewater Creek. There is a day-use picnic area at the bridge with toilet facilities, parking, and garbage cans, but no drinking water. A few hundred yards upstream is an undeveloped campground where you can park your RV or pitch a tent. It is sort of level, but there are no facilities.

If you want improved camping facilities, water, toilets, tables and so on, travel about 5 miles north to South Bluewater State Park or 8 miles south on Forest Roads 178 and 480 to Ojo Redondo Campground near Post Office Flat. Otherwise, go in search of a suitable pull-off and just make do.

Bluewater Lake

Location: Zuni Mountains, Cibola National Forest
Maps: Cibola NF Visitors Map, Zuni/Mt. Taylor Ranger Districts; Zuni title, USGS 1:100,000 series
Elevation: 7,500 feet
Size: 1,600 acres
Best Times: spring and fall
Fish Species: rainbow trout, channel catfish, suckers
Contributed by: George Sanders

Bluewater Lake is formed by a concrete arch dam built in 1927 at the confluence of Bluewater and Cottonwood Creeks. This lake is located just east of the Continental Divide in a high basin at 7,500 feet elevation in the Zuni Mountain Range, one of the rare east-to-west-oriented mountain systems. For decades Bluewater Lake has yielded some of the largest rainbow trout in the state, including a 16-pound state record.

To access the west shore take the Thoreau Exit from I-40 and follow NM 612 south for 10 miles. For the east shore, (damsite) take the Prewitt Exit and follow NM 412 for 5 miles. State Parks and camping are located on both sides.

Unfortunately the lake lives and dies on snowmelt from the 9,000-foot ridges to the south. Throughout the 1970s and early 1980s the lake levels were consistently high and the fishing was very good on average. Primarily a put-and-take fishery with some holdovers, the lake produced large and numerous stringers of trout and catfish. In the mid to late 1980s the area had successive drought years and high irrigation pull-downs. This caused a gradual decline in the water levels and a high, winter kill, due to shallow reserves.

Another result of the low water levels was poor aquatic plant mass. With full lake levels, the water clarity was excellent, allowing for light penetration and great plant growth, especially in the shallow Cottonwood arm. The surrounding watershed has seen considerable clearcut logging, contributing to siltation.

The food sources in Bluewater Lake are typical of cool-water lakes. Scuds, snails, leeches, and crayfish offer large prey. Among the insects present are both dragonflies and damselflies, even with an absence of tule reeds and cattails. There are some mayflies, and an occasional caddis, but this is mainly a subsurface lake for the fly fisher.

Bluewater Lake is readily fished from a raft or float tube in the Cottonwood arm. In late September and October the pondweed and milfoil have died back, and slowly stripped or trolled streamers are productive. The same tactic will work in the spring, after ice-out, but before the runoff has made the lake murky and unsettled. The midsummer months are hectic with recreational boaters. You'll be sharing the lake with both ski boats and jet skis.

Nutria Lakes
Location: Zuni Indian Reservation
Maps: Cibola NF Visitors Map, Zuni/Mt. Taylor Ranger Districts; Zuni title, USGS 1:100,000 series
Size: 480 acres
Best Times: spring
Fish Species: rainbow trout and yellow perch
Contributed by: George Sanders

Nutria Lake #2, located on the Zuni Indian Reservation, can be described as a 2-mile-long open marsh. Nutria Creek begins at about 8,000 feet in the Zuni Mountains, 20 miles to the northeast, then drops off the range through a series of canyons until it reaches upper Nutria village. Here the Zuni people began to farm the valley many centuries ago. The lake is formed by a low earthen dam across the lower valley. This impoundment stores runoff for downstream farming in and around Zuni Pueblo, 15 miles to the southwest. The lake is shallow, averaging 8 to 10 feet deep, and is exceedingly clear.

When full in the spring and early summer, Nutria Lake is 3 miles long and approximately a quarter-mile wide, ringed with marsh grass and tule reeds. In the middle and upper end the tule and cattails extend from side to side, leaving channels and islands for the small boat or float tubers to navigate. The filtering process of this long wetland system must account for the clarity of the water. It is so clear, in fact, that some have snorkeled this lake observing the trout.

The Zuni tribe stocks this lake and several others on the reservation, including another lake in the same drainage 2 miles upstream called Nutria #4; this is more of a hillside body of water. The ecology of the two lakes is completely different. The upper lake is formed by damming a side arroyo. It has a larger open-water area, surrounded by piñon-juniper hills and outcroppings. The lower lake is like the Bosque Del Apache with rainbow trout—a float tuber's paradise.

Fishing permits are $6/day and are available from the Zuni Tribal Finance Office, venders in Zuni, Charlie's Sporting Goods in Albuquerque, and others. The bag limit is 10 trout.

The best times to fish Nutria #2 are from late April to mid-June when the irrigation season begins to lower the lake level and the water temperature passes 60 degrees. For float tube fishing, a sinking line is unnecessary. A long leader 9 to 12 feet in length, 6x–7x tippets, and a slow retrieve will cover any fish holding areas. One good tactic for catching those fish hunting the edge of the reed beds is to station the tube 20 to 30 feet out in the open water and cast back against the reeds. One can cast within 1 or 2 feet of the reeds without fear of hanging up. Unlike milfoil or hyacinth, these stands don't taper off with submerged plants, but terminate in a vertical wall that is often 6 feet deep at the edge.

These trout average 8 to 12 inches and will take any small dry attractor such as an Elk Hair Caddis, Double Hackle Peacock, or Griffith's Gnat. When trout are feeding, the fly will work either cast on the surface or stripped back when drowned. Smaller streamers, such as Peacock Woolly Worms, Prince Nymphs, and Damselfly Nymphs, also work well. These should be tied no larger then 10 or 12 on a barbless hook. The barbless hook enables one to reload faster during one of these feeding binges. This lake is not challenging technically, but is the ideal venue to break in a novice in the art of float-tube fishing.

Nutria Lake is also home to a healthy population of yellow perch. They occasionally will strike caddisflies and any popping-bug-type fly. For bird watchers, there are large nesting populations of coots, moorhens, and red-winged blackbirds. I've seen western grebes and migrating mergansers, as well. Camping is not allowed at the lower lake due to the proximity of sensitive archeological sites. The Great Kiva, an Anasazi ruin, is within walking distance of the lake. The lower lake is 3.5 miles from NM 602 on a good gravel-surfaced road. The turnoff is well marked between 2 and 3 miles north of its terminus with NM 53.

Ramah Lake

Location: Zuni Mountains

Maps: Cibola NF Visitors Map, Zuni/Mt. Taylor Ranger Districts; Zuni title, USGS 1:100,000 series

Elevation: 6,000 feet

Size: 100 acres

Best Times: spring and fall

Fish Species: rainbow trout, bass, bluegill

Contributed by: George Sanders

Ramah Lake is located just off NM 53 north of the village of Ramah, a farming community on the southern edge of the Zuni Mountains. The lake, managed by the Ramah Irrigation District until about 1986, was built for irrigation and was not a popular public fishery until recently, when the New Mexico Department of Game and Fish secured an agreement to stock and manage the lake for public access and fishing. Catchable-sized rainbow trout averaging 12 inches are stocked, but a large portion hold over and many 20-inch-plus rainbows have been taken.

The lake lies in a narrow valley shaped like a dogleg. The one-third of the lake near the earthen dam is oriented east to west, with the upper two-thirds oriented northeast to southwest. The depth of the lake and its 6,000-foot elevation keep it mostly ice-free and prevent winter kill. The lake is bordered on the north in the inside of the dogleg by a high, sheer, sandstone promontory that prevents travel along the shoreline on that side. The opposite side of the lower lake is a gentler, piñon-juniper hillside, much like the Quemado Lake topography. The upper two-thirds of the lake is quite shallow and fringed with reeds and cat-tails, backing up into a gently sloped meadow.

The preferred mode of fishing in Ramah Lake is to deep-troll the lower lake and bank-fish the dam area. Electric motors are allowed and many anglers from Albuquerque frequent the lake in season.

Of interest to the fly fisherman is the fact that the upper part of the lake is very productive in the spring and fall, when the reed beds and some embayments are fished from a small boat or float tube. Wade-fishing in the lake is nearly impossible, due to the depth in the lower lake and the thickness of the reeds in the upper lake. Also, the lake bottom in the upper lake is composed of black silt and organic matter that will suck your waders off your feet.

The most successful patterns are the small streamer flies, including Woolly Buggers in green and black, Marabou Leech patterns, damsel nymphs, and large Peacock Double Hackles fished wet. These flies must be presented from open water toward the reeds. This axiom holds true for all except the damsel, which should be presented in the opposite fashion.

One note on weather: in the spring and fall, when the prevailing westerly wind is very strong, those who put in at the dam access may experience difficulty returning from the upper section of the lake. If one is in a float tube or under oar power, it may be necessary to wait out the gusts and continue fishing in the calmer upper lake, and then round the promontory during a lull in the wind. Often the fishing continues good in the upper end when the bravest troller has packed it in near the dam.

McGaffey Lake

Location: Zuni Mountains
Maps: Cibola NF Visitors Map, Zuni/Mt. Taylor Ranger Districts; Zuni title, USGS 1:100,000 series
Elevation: 8,000 feet
Size: 14 acres
Best Times: spring
Fish Species: rainbow trout
Contributed by: George Sanders

McGaffey Lake sits at an elevation of over 8,000 feet in the Zuni Mountains near Gallup, New Mexico. The lake is at the end of NM 400, 10 miles south of I-40. Take the McGaffey Exit.

The lake is between 10 and 15 acres, depending upon the time of year. In spring it is swelled with snowmelt and water from the numerous springs in the meadow above it. The lake is stocked with rainbow trout in spring and summer, providing good fishing until late summer, when moss and low water levels take effect.

McGaffey Lake is very popular with bait and artificial lure fishers from the Gallup area. The location of good picnic and camping areas just down the road from the lake ensures crowds throughout the warmer months.

For the fly fisher, the lake is worth a visit in the spring until June, when the water temperature rises and the fish become less active. Although small craft are allowed, the most effective method to fish McGaffey Lake is with a float tube in the upper portion, where one will find a border of cattails across the entire upper lake. In spring the fish feed near the margins of the cattails and can be taken on dry flies such as olive Elk Hair Caddis, Renegade, and Griffith's Gnats. Any peacock-body fly, be it a streamer such as a Peacock and Gray or a Double Hackle fished dry, will produce.

In the early summer evenings, one can do well on McGaffey Lake with a Blue-winged Olive or a Parachute Adams near the reeds. By midsummer the fishing pressure, water temperature, and water level make the trip less attractive for fly fishers.

CHAPTER FOURTEEN

Other Waters

Rio Grande

Location: central New Mexico downstream from Elephant Butte
Maps: Truth or Consequences title, USGS 1:100,000 series
Elevation: 4,200 feet
Length: 8 miles
Best Times: November–April
Fish Species: rainbow trout

The Rio Grande from Elephant Butte Reservoir to Williamsburg, New Mexico, is managed as a winter trout water, with catchable rainbows planted from November through March. The water flow is controlled for crop irrigation, and there is little water in the river during the winter trout season. This section of the Rio Grande flows for 8 miles from Elephant Butte Dam southwest, along the southeastern side of Truth or Consequences and Williamsburg, and then south into Caballo Reservoir.

With the low flows, most of the stocked trout are removed from the river in a very short time. Those trout that aren't caught immediately grow at a fantastic rate, as the river is very fertile. By summer some 16-inch fish may be found. When there were several years of year-round flows of cold water from Elephant Butte Reservoir, 8- to 11-pound rainbow trout were caught. Trout can live in this part of the river during the high irrigation flows of summer, but fishing for trout during these high flows is difficult. When the irrigation flow is cut off in the fall in some years, the fishing can be good for a few days until the fish are caught, or the water becomes too warm.

Except for a few years when high water caused year-round flow in the Rio Grande at Truth or Consequences, it has not become popular with fly fishers. This could change when a continuous supply of water is supplied to El Paso. The Rio Grande below Elephant Butte Reservoir has the potential to be a good tailwater trout fishery, except during extended droughts when the water in the lake may get too warm.

This tailwater has good hatches of *Baetis* (Blue-winged Olive) and *Tricorythodes* (Trico) mayflies. I have seen the water covered with mayfly spinners. Caddisflies and *Diptera* (midge) are common in the Rio Grande. The river also contains aquatic worms. When there were many large trout in the river, Zonkers were popular flies that imitated the bait-fish common to this part of the river.

Other Waters

There are a few other trout spots in New Mexico south of I-40 that are worth looking into. Tajique Canyon, in the Cibola National Forest on the eastern slope of the Manzano Mountains, contains stocked rainbow trout in some 4 miles of water at the 7,400- to 6,800-foot elevation range, between Fourth of July and Tajique Campgrounds. It is reachable via Forest Road 55 from the village of Tajique, which lies on NM 14, south of Albuquerque. Nearby Torreon Canyon, also reachable via FR 55, has some potential habitat. A bit farther south, Manzano Pond lies near the village of the same name on NM 14 and is also stocked by NMG&F with rainbows. It is open to bank-fishing during the day.

Roadless, trail-less, extremely rugged North McKittrick Canyon flows across the state line from New Mexico's Lincoln National Forest into Texas's Guadalupe Mountains National Park. It holds green sunfish and possibly a few of the naturalized rainbows from the big springs in Mckittrick Canyon, into which it flows. If you catch a trout in the New Mexico part of the stream, you may have been the first even to fish it. The park waters in Texas are close by, but closed to fishing.

Appendix

Important Aquatic Insects of the Gila National Forest

Ephemeroptera (Mayflies)
Species Specific Information
Scientific name: *Baetis* sp.
Common name: Blue-winged Olive
Patterns: Baetis, Hare's Ear #16 (nymph); Dark Blue Quill or Blue-winged
Olive Dun #16; Blue Quill Spinner #16
Time of hatch: emerges sporadically in summer, fall, and winter afternoons
Watersheds: all

Scientific name: Ephemerella infrequens and inermis
Common name: Pale Morning Dun
Patterns: Hare's Ear, Pheasant Tail, Pale Morning Dun (nymphs) #14–16; Pale
Morning Dun Hendrickson, Adams, Tan Sparkle Dun (duns) #14–16; Female
Hendrickson, Rusty Polywing (spinner) #14–16
Time of hatch: emerges early summer through July, mid-mornings through
afternoon
Watersheds: Gila Mainstem, East Fork

Scientific name: *Heptagenia* sp.
Common name: Pale Evening Dun
Patterns: Gold-ribbed Hare's Ear, Iron Nymph, Zug Bug (nymphs) #14–16;
Green Paradrake, Adams, Pale Evening Dun (duns) #14–16; spinners not
important
Time of hatch: summer evenings
Watersheds: Gila system: Mimbres, Blue

Scientific name: *Paraleptophlebia* sp.
Common name: Mahogany Dun or Blue Dun
Patterns: Leptophlebia, Hare's Ear, Bird's Nest, Pheasant Tail (nymphs)
#12–18; Iron Blue, Red Quill, Dark Blue Quill (duns) #12–18; Blue Quill,
Brown Polywing (spinners) #12–18
Time of hatch: summer afternoons
Watersheds: Gila system: Middle Fork, Mimbres, Blue

Scientific name: *Tricorythodes* sp.
Common name: Trico
Patterns: Black No Hackle (dun) #20; Trico (spinner) #20
Time of hatch: mid-morning in spring and summer
Watersheds: Gila system: Mimbres, San Francisco, Blue

Plecoptera (Stoneflies)
Species Specific Information
Scientific name: *Isoperla* sp. and *Alloperla* sp.
Common name: Little Yellow Stonefly
Patterns: Little Yellow Stonefly #10; Marabou Muddler #8–10
Time of hatch: summer mornings
Watersheds: Gila system, except East Fork Mainstem; San Francisco

Scientific name: *Skwala* sp.
Common name: Golden Stonefly, Yellow Stonefly
Patterns: Golden Stone, Little Yellow Stone (nymphs) #8–10
Time of hatch: late spring, all day
Watersheds: Middle Fork, West Fork system, Diamond Creek system

Scientific name: *Ampinemura* sp.
Common name: Little Brown Stonefly
Patterns: Little Brown Stonefly Nymph #10
Time of hatch: early summer mornings
Watersheds: Mimbres, Blue, Diamond Creek

Tricoptera (Caddisflies)
Species Specific Information
Scientific name: *Hydropsyche* sp.
Common name: Spotted Sedge
Patterns: Rockworm (larva) #12–16; Green Sparkle, Bird's Nest (pupa)
#12–16; Elk Hair Caddis, Adams (adult) #12–16
Time of hatch: summer evenings
Watersheds: all

Scientific name: *Hydroptila* sp.
Common name: Microcaddis
Patterns: Tan Soft Hackle (pupa) #18–22; Tan Soft Hackle (adult) #18–22
Time of hatch: summer evenings
Watersheds: Gila Mainstem

Scientific name: *Glossoma* sp.
Common name: Turtle Casemaker and Saddle Casemaker
Patterns: Turtle Casemaker, Bird's Nest, Copper-ribbed Rusty (pupa) #16–18;
Elk Hair Caddis, Soft Hackle (adult) #16–18
Time of hatch: summer evenings
Watersheds: Gila Mainstem, Middle Fork, Mimbres, Blue

Scientific name: *Leptoceridae* family
Common name: Horn Casemaker
Patterns: Hare's Ear Beadhead, Strawman, Peeking Caddis (larva) #12–16;
Black Sparkle (pupa) #12–16; Elk Hair Caddis (adult) #12–16
Time of hatch: all day
Watersheds: Gila Mainstem, Middle, West Fork, San Francisco tributaries

Diptera (Midges)
Familes: Chironomidae and Simuliidae
Common names: Midges and Blackflies
Patterns: Cream, Black, Gray, or Green Midge (larva) #18–24; Cream, Black,
Gray, or Green Midge (pupa) #18–24; Dun, Green, or Black Midge (adult)
#18–24
Time of hatch: May to October, sporadic
Watersheds: all

Megaloptera (Dobsonflies)
Family: Corydalidae
Common name: Dobsonflies
Patterns: Olive, Purple, Brown, and Black Woolly Buggers (larva) #6–10
Time of hatch: not applicable (pupates on land)
Watersheds: Gila Mainstem, Middle Fork

Ondonata (Damselflies and Dragonflies)
Genus Specific Information
Genus: Ophiogomphus
Common name: Green Darner
Patterns: Green Darner Dragonfly #8
Time of hatch: all summer
Watersheds: all
Genus: Enallagma
Common name: Blue Damsel
Patterns: Blue Damsel #8
Time of hatch: all summer
Watersheds: San Francisco

Index